THE STANDING OF EUROPE IN THE NEW IMPERIAL WORLD ORDER

A Convoco Edition

CORINNE MICHAELA FLICK (ED.)

Convoco! Editions

Copyright © for the texts by the authors
and Convoco Foundation 2020

The rights of the named authors to be identified as the authors of this work have been asserted in accordance with the Copyright, Designs and Patents Act, 1988.

The publisher has used its best endeavors to ensure that the URLs for external websites referred to in this book are correct and active at the time of going to press. However, the publisher has no responsibility for the websites and can make no guarantee that a site will remain live or that the content is or will remain appropriate.

Convoco Foundation
Brienner Strasse 28
D – 80333 Munich
www.convoco.co.uk

British Library Cataloguing-in-Publication data: a catalogue record for this book is available from the British Library.

Edited by Dr. Corinne Michaela Flick
Translated from German by Philippa Hurd
Layout and typesetting by Jill Sawyer Phypers
Printed and bound in Great Britain by Clays Ltd., St Ives plc

ISBN: 978-1-9163673-0-2

Previously published Convoco titles:

The Multiple Futures of Capitalism (2019)

The Common Good in the 21st Century (2018)

Authority in Transformation (2017)

Power and its Paradoxes (2016)

To Do or Not To Do—Inaction as a Form of Action (2015)

Dealing with Downturns: Strategies in Uncertain Times (2014)

Collective Law-Breaking—A Threat to Liberty (2013)

Who Owns the World's Knowledge? (2012)

Can't Pay, Won't Pay? Sovereign Debt and the Challenge of Growth in Europe (2011)

It is the duty of a patriot to prefer and promote the exclusive interest and glory of his native country; but a philosopher may be permitted to enlarge his views, and to consider Europe as one great republic, whose various inhabitants have attained almost the same level of politeness and cultivation. The balance of power will continue to fluctuate, and the prosperity of our own, or the neighbouring kingdoms, may be alternately exalted or depressed; but these partial events cannot essentially injure our general state of happiness, the system of arts, and laws, and manners, which so distinguish the Europeans.

Edward Gibbon (1737–1794)

CONTENTS

Introduction		1
Theses		19

1. Europe: Ideas of Unity and a Sense of Crisis
   Jörn Leonhard — 27

2. European Legal Identities and European Legal Identity
   Birke Häcker — 45

3. Where is Europe Going? An Appeal for More Diversity in the European Union
   Stefan Korioth — 65

4. Why Nationalism—A European Identity
   Yael Tamir — 79

5. European Values and Good Leadership: 97
   Facing up to Role Distance
   Timo Meynhardt

6. Making Better Use of Europe's Great 119
   Potential
   Stefan Oschmann

7. Europe's Strategic Autonomy in Digital 135
   Technologies: Pipe Dream or
   Realistic Vision?
   Roberto Viola

8. Europe, What is to be Done? The EU 147
   Between Old Myths and New Challenges
   Sven Simon

9. NATO and Europe's Strategic Autonomy 167
   Kai A. Konrad

10. European Identity in Challenging Times: 179
    Advocating the European Success Model
    with Confidence
    Claudia Wiesner

11. New Views of Familiar Terrain 199
    Hans Ulrich Obrist and Edi Rama
    in Conversation

12. Rethink Markets: Criteria for an Agile   225
    Competition Policy
    Matthias Karl

13. Freedom is not the Absence of Regulation   245
    In Conversation with Rupprecht Podszun

14. How Should Germany and Europe Deal   253
    with the Growing Importance of China?
    Jörg Rocholl

15. The Asian Century   267
    In Conversation with Parag Khanna

16. Europe and the Global Economic Order   273
    Gabriel Felbermayr

17. The End of an Era, the Beginning of   297
    a New: Structural Change in the
    European Economy
    Fredrik Erixon

18. On the Value of Europe's Diversity   311
    Christoph G. Paulus

Contributors   327

INTRODUCTION

Dear Friends of Convoco,

For the first time in its 15-year history of enquiry and debate, Convoco is turning its attention towards the condition of Europe. Of course, we have been discussing Europe, albeit indirectly, since our inception. This has been almost inevitable. Whenever we consider the rule of law, or the workings of democracy, or when we examine the idea of the common good and its manifestation in the welfare state, we are necessarily drawn to the experience of Europe. Although these principles are subject to differences in interpretation and practice across the continent, they are nevertheless all values that are central to Europe's political order and social experience. Moreover, one can say without exaggeration that Europe has been the source of many of the ideas and concepts that are now regarded as essential to the world's civilization—at which point we are already halfway to providing answers to the questions raised in the present book: what has Europe to offer the world? What does Europe stand for? And what justifies Europe's claim to be a global player alongside the USA and the emerging great powers of Asia?

Yet we are faced with a paradox. At the very point when European ideas are globally at their most influential, belief in Europe and what it has to offer the world seems to be disappearing within Europe itself. The "European idea"—and the optimism of the founders of what has since become the European Union—is not *en vogue* at present. We look on as our era descends into turmoil: anger, confusion, prejudice, and the radicalization of people who were not radical before. Europe has lost confidence in itself—consider the United Kingdom's exit from the EU and the growth of nationalism in individual countries. Nothing seems certain any more, after Western Europe has lived through 70 years of unparalleled prosperity and the absence of war.

Europe, with its Christian roots and its Enlightenment principles, is undergoing an identity crisis. Of course, the "idea of Europe" has constantly been re-shaped and re-negotiated throughout its history. To this day Europe's motto (adopted in 2000) "united in diversity" is an idea that is waiting to be implemented in reality. The key question here is how to create a unity out of the diversity of European nations, a unity in which each nation can lead its own individual life, while at the same time limiting its sovereignty to the extent that makes it possible to act internationally in unity. It is about creating unity through diversity and differences, and not imposing a unity on the plurality. It is about coexistence based on cooperation. Such a Europe emerges through the mutual appreciation of otherness;[1] and this, in turn, means recognizing the identity of others, from whom one wants to distinguish oneself by asserting one's own identity.

Culturally, Europe has been shaped by the spirit of Christianity, which can be traced back to Greco-Roman and Jewish traditions. But these ideas have been profoundly re-shaped by the legacy of the European Enlightenment in the 17th and 18th centuries, which imposed bounds on the power of the Church and its capacity to rule individuals' behavior and consciences. Europe, in its stand for personal freedom, democracy, and the rights of the individual, is very much the heir to this historical tradition. The constitutional guarantee of individual civil liberties, for example, emerged in England in the 17th century. The aim of the constitutional state is the moderation of state power, the granting of fundamental and human rights, and the self-determination and right of citizens to seek judicial protection. Arguably, the greatest achievement of the Enlightenment is the separation of Church and state. Only the secular state made it possible for science to establish its authority, while the Christian principles of charity, brotherhood, and humility—not just Marxist centralism as it often seems from the other side of the Atlantic—are reflected in the modern welfare state.

It would be naive, of course, to suggest that Europe's historical influence on the world has been universally benign. While tolerance, freedom, and justice were established on the continent, European imperialism and colonialism—with all that these involved by way of oppression, slavery, and rejection of the other, founded in a sense of European superiority—existed at the same time. As with most states and empires, an integral feature of Europe is that it is based on the one hand on the principle of inclusion, and on the other hand on the principle of exclusion. From the 17th century, the political and social development of the continent took place mainly in contradistinction to non-European cultures. Historically, "the foreign" was excluded as primitive, wild, and exotic.

From the late 18th century, Europe began to re-acquire a stronger European consciousness: a sense of collective identity which had been profoundly disrupted by the Reformation in the 16th and 17th centuries, and which found political expression in the attempt to establish a workable pan-European order at the Congress of Vienna in 1815, in the aftermath of the defeat of Napoleon. All areas of society were conceived as sharing large parts of one vision: economic and social systems, fashion, architecture, science, and technological progress. This European consciousness interpreted its own identity as historically rooted and culturally determined by contrasting it with real and fictitious images. These constructions of cultural otherness served on the one hand to encourage critical self-examination and on the other as a means of self-differentiation united in the face of the outside world.[2]

This modern European consciousness can perhaps be summed up in the words of the great French historian Jean-Baptiste Duroselle (1917–1994): *"L'Europe face aux Turcs. L'Europe face à l'Amérique. L'Europe face à elle-même."*[3] This was a historic characterization of Europe that had already been reflected in the paintings of Peter Paul Rubens in the early 17th century. On the one hand, Rubens depicted Christian Europe as threatened by the Orient: the global Muslim empire and the Ottoman threat had acted as the "identity-creating other" for Christians since the fall of Constantinople in 1453. On the other hand, Rubens also documented Europe's destruction of itself through its internal power struggles and confessional wars. Throughout that century, Europe lived through just three individual years without military conflict, and the yearning for peace was as strong and urgent as it was to be again in the 20th century.

Like the post-Westphalian Europe that emerged from the disaster of the Thirty Years War, the Europe of today has been shaped by the conflicts that dominated the first half of the 20th century—and by the idealism that grew out of the ashes of 1945. To the age-old European ideas of the Enlightenment were added the concepts of what has since become the European Union: the Single Market, equality of treatment before the law, and citizenship of a continent-wide European Union. Among these principles, the Single Market is the secure and powerful achievement. The EU is the world's largest economy, with a gross national product of €31,000 per capita of 500 million consumers. At the same time, it is the world's largest trading bloc. However, the Single Market alone cannot create identity. The European Union, and therefore Europe, is "in need of meaning," as today's EU has followed an economic path, rather than a cultural one.

Back in 1986, the German poet and commentator Hans Magnus Enzensberger wrote: "...The propagandists of the single market [have over time] divested themselves of all Western pretensions. Interests have taken the place of ideas... The 'idea' that was once preached so forcefully has become dispensable."[4]

Today, there is just one clear narrative of values, namely Europe as a peace project. Historically, the unification of Germany in 1871 created at the heart of the European states a nation that was too big, too economically strong, and too powerful to find a counterbalance within the continent. The collapse of this fragile European balance led to the two world wars. A desire for peace arose that went beyond the various European national borders. Thus, the "German Question" has shaped the Europe of today and is the reason behind the creation of a number of European institutions, from the European Steel and Coal Community to today's European Union. Therefore, the importance of Europe as a peace project has been repeatedly emphasized. But as Europe's military conflicts recede ever further into the past, the narrative of values promoting European peace seems increasingly to slip from view.

There is, therefore, an urgent need to come up with additional meaningful narratives in order to create the kind of Europe-wide social cohesion that is grounded, not just in economic interest, but also in emotional commitment—the very sentiment that is so easily appealed to by anti-EU nationalists. Historically, it has always been collective narratives, whether based on reality or fiction, that have brought societies together and through which has emerged a sense of belonging. People think in stories, not in facts, numbers, and statistics, and the simpler the story, very often the more effective it is.[5] Europe itself started as a literary motif. The name "Europa" first appears in Homer's *Iliad*, then in the 5th century BCE Herodotus chose the name to designate the countries north of the Mediterranean that were not part of Asia.

Such a meaningful narrative for Europe might, for example, be the nobility of the welfare state (and hence the imperative to preserve it for the future). Until now, each individual state has been responsible for ensuring a balance between democracy, capitalism, and social security, and is valued by its citizens for doing so. This successful model is coming under increasing pressure as a result of demographic change. The nation state is encountering more and more ever-increasing problems regarding the effective protection of its citizens. A European community of welfare solidarity—meaning that the welfare state is no longer connected to the nation but to the union—might be a remedy for this situation.[6] The feeling of Europe being a welfare community could eventually strengthen a feeling of compassion among European neighbors. It must be noted, however, that without greater fiscal and economic convergence among EU states, there will be a risk of new European tensions if the economically more productive countries feel that the less successful are benefiting unfairly from such a welfare system.

Democracy is also important for Europe's overall narrative. As a common value, it played a crucial role in the creation of modern European identity. It was and is the connecting transatlantic bond as well. Historically, the culmination was the fall of the Berlin Wall in 1989 and the founding of the European Union in 1993. This new Europe is the answer to 20th-century nationalism. It has produced a willingness to share sovereignty and to exercise power collectively. Today's Europe, and today's Germany in particular, are both products of this liberal world order.

The crisis of our own times is that this liberal order suddenly seems to be in danger because it has no answers to the major challenges of our time: climate change and technological disruption, which both go hand-in-hand with economic polarization. Globally, the liberal narrative is also in crisis. And this crisis is causing people to return to old ideas that have already been proved wrong in the 20th century, such as nationalism, religious fanaticism, or the socialism of the last century. So Europe has a dual problem. On the one hand there is a lack of meaningful narratives; on the other hand, liberalism, a fundamental component of Europe's value-system, is in global crisis.

In Eastern Europe, we are confronted with the transformation of recent democratic governments, such as those of Hungary and Poland, into illiberal, authoritarian systems. In the South, populism and the economic divergence of Greece and Italy are threatening. In the West, Europe is losing an important Member State. Strong populist tendencies can be observed in varying degrees throughout Europe. The landscape of political parties is shifting seriously and destabilizing governments.

Europe is in a transitional stage between a system of independent nation states and a united Europe—even if the ultimate extent of that European unification remains a subject of controversy. Such periods of transformation are usually unsettling and entail a loss of orientation. Moreover, factors that helped create the cultural framework within which a united Europe was first projected—such as first-hand experiences of the horrors experienced in the first half of the 20th century—are receding with time.

Transitions require shared cultural experiences or even shared rituals—and that is precisely what we lack. We should spend more time thinking about what constitutes Europe culturally, and then create rituals that help Europe to be united. For example, the members of the EU should put more emphasis on celebrating the annual "Europe Day" on May 9; the DiscoverEU internal program could be expanded, providing train tickets for school graduates to allow them to visit the other European countries similar to the "gap year" in Anglo-Saxon countries.[7] The European idea needs emotion, and European citizens must be able to feel enthusiastic about it, as only then will a common feeling of European identity emerge.

Building on an established European identity, we should then consider whether a greater unity is not a necessary precondition if Europe is to be a global player. The geopolitical strategist Parag Khanna is one of many commentators to describe the 21st century as the "century of Asia."[8] After many years of colonialism and division as a result of the Cold War, a measure of cohesion is once again returning to Asia. Asia's economies have been growing for years. Asian domestic trade, seen as part of overall trade in Asia, almost doubled from 29 percent to 57 percent between 2009 and 2016. Not just the individual economies, but the entire Asian region is strengthening as a unified trading area. The rapid development of these trading relationships within and between the non-Western regions constitutes a major new development, and one which lessens and, in some cases, removes their earlier dependency on the USA and Europe.

This means that Europe is now facing two strong trading areas: one to its west, and another to the east. The "America First" policy of the current US government is pressuring the EU towards stronger autonomy, both militarily and economically. At the same time, American protectionism is provoking Europe and Asia to build new trade relationships of their own. And looking to the near future, we should not lose sight of Africa. Africa has established a continental free-trade area, known as CFTA. If it is successful, it will create a market of 1.3 billion people today, with an annual economic output of 2 trillion euros.[9]

It seems that to operate as an effective global player capable of dealing with global political challenges, Europe must develop a much greater degree of political unity. This point is even more important if Europe is to deal effectively with the new global mega-companies such as Amazon, Alphabet, Apple, and Facebook, because they too are part of the "new imperial world order."

Here Europe starts at a relative disadvantage. For it should also be noted that Europe's economic innovations in the field of digitalization are a long way behind the attainments of the Silicon Valley mega-corporations. In asking why this should be so, a question arises as to whether, and to what extent, the values and concepts that currently make for Europe's uniqueness represent an obstacle in this new and technologically competitive world. How must these values be adapted, if necessary, to smooth Europe's progress through the new century and the new millennium?

Let me give one example of such an adaptation, by focusing on the rule of law. As is well known, the law is a fundamental way of limiting the uncertainty of the future. Legally binding agreements make the future more predictable. But a great deal of uncertainty remains, and this very uncertainty is a basic requirement of capitalist economies, as it opens up opportunities for innovation and creativity. Indeed, uncertainty can be seen as the constitutive condition of capitalist economies. In light of this fact, we may ask whether Europe has taken the rule of law in the economic sphere too far. We should consider whether the rule of law—at least in Europe's Western democracies—has become an obstacle to innovation. An excessive burden of regulation is one of the main and recurrent criticisms of the EU. And in this we can see yet another reason for Brexit.

But we must not forget that the rule of law is one of the most important features of European identity and is a requirement of our ability to live together in freedom. It is crucial to recognize that only traffic regulations and their enforcement enable the free movement of equal road users. As has been debated endlessly since the days of Solon, there is a fine line between a legal system that oppresses society and constricts the economy and one that promotes well-being and innovation. A strong state and a strong society must find a balance so that freedom—including freedom for technological and economic innovation—can flourish.[10]

The rule of law is the precondition of all fundamental and human rights. At the presentation of the International Charlemagne Prize in May 2019, António Guterres said: "Europe is too meaningful to fail," because that would also be a "failure of a world in which the rule of law can prevail... As Secretary General of the United Nations now, I never felt so clearly the need of a strong and united Europe."[11]

There are reasons for some optimism. The project of a united Europe has not failed yet. In the past, Europe has shown that it can change and that it has the ability to redefine itself. Throughout history, Europe has always evolved. Through adaptation and change, it has negotiated the difficulties that always attend periods of transition. Only one thing so far seems sure: it cannot go on with its current structures and modes of deliberation unchanged.

In 2013, Convoco debated the topic *Dealing with Downturns: Strategies in Uncertain Times*. Only the imprudent do not factor in the possibility of failure. The wise know that failure, and the need to learn from these experiments, is part of successful actions. The philosopher Karl Popper showed science how to make discoveries via a failed attempt. Science recognizes the principle of trial and error. Let's apply it to the European project.

Ultimately, the need for unity exists not only in relation to Europe, but also to the world community itself. How can we face up to challenges such as climate change other than as a far more cooperative network of states that recognizes a universal community of interests? The answer can only be a new global order that will create a common, more cooperative, and more integrated international system. That should be the goal of us all.

Notes

1. Cf. Bazon Brock, "Europa fällt" in *Die Welt*, May 5, 2019; Bazon Brock, "Europa bleibt" in *Die Welt*, May 24, 2019.
2. Nicolas Detering, *Krise und Kontinent: Die Entstehung der deutschen Europa-Literatur in der Frühen Neuzeit* (Cologne: Böhlau Verlag, 2017), p. 542.
3. Jean-Baptiste Duroselle, *L'idée d'Europe dans l'histoire* (Paris: Denoël, 1965), pp. 75–103.
4. Hans Magnus Enzensberger, "Brüssel oder Europa – eins von beiden" in Hans Magnus Enzensberger (ed.), *Der fliegende Robert* (Frankfurt am Main: Suhrkamp, 1989), p. 118.
5. Yuval Noah Harari, "Does Trump's Rise Mean Liberalism's End?" in *The New Yorker*, October 8, 2016.
6. A study carried out by Gerhards et al. found a majority of people across Europe had a positive opinion of the idea of a Europe-wide community of solidarity: Jürgen Gerhards, Zsófia S. Ignácz, Florian K. Kley, Holger Lengfeld, and Maximilian Priem, "How Strong is European Welfare Solidarity? Results from a Comparative Survey conducted in 13 EU Member States" in Martin Heidenreich (ed.). *Horizontal Europeanisation. The Transnationalisation of Daily Life and Social Fields in Europe* (New York: Routledge, 2019), pp. 39–57.
7. One of the reasons why European identity is strongest among young people is that their social and cultural horizons have been widened by first-hand experience of other European states. See Sarah Ciaglia, Clemens Fuest & Friedrich Heinemann, "What a Feeling!? How to Promote

European Identity," *ifo Institute and Centre for Economic Research*, July 18, 2018, pp. 23–24.

8. Parag Khanna, *The Future is Asian: Global Order in the Twenty-First Century* (London: Weidenfeld & Nicolson, 2019); see also the Convoco interview with Parag Khanna in this volume.

9. Bundesministerium für Wirtschaft und Energie, "Die panafrikanische Freihandelszone AfCFTA – der Weg zu einem integrierten, aufstrebenden und friedlicheren Afrika?," September 3, 2019, https://www.bmwi.de/Redaktion/DE/ Schlaglichter-der-Wirtschaftspolitik/2019/09/kapitel-1- 6-pan-afrikanische-freihandelszone.html (accessed January 14, 2020).

10. See Daron Acemoglu and James A. Robinson, *The Narrow Corridor: States, Societies and the Fate of Liberty* (London: Penguin Press, 2019).

11. António Guterres, "Address at the International Charlemagne Prize of Aachen for the Unity of Europe," May 30, 2019, https://www.un.org/sg/en/content/sg/speeches /2019-05-30/address-international-charlemagne-prize-of -aachen-for-unity-of-europe (accessed October 16, 2019).

THESES

STEFAN OSCHMANN

We need a European Union that is a leader in science and technology, and whose researchers and entrepreneurs rank among global technology leaders. Such a Europe will flourish, ensure the prosperity of its citizens, and play a role in shaping the world of the 21st century.

CHRISTOPH G. PAULUS

By comparison with the US and China, Europe appears to be falling behind as a result of its diversity. A shared uniformity of appearance and action is lacking throughout. But maybe we can find strength in this dissonance, and such examples already exist.

EDI RAMA

The thing is this: what brings us all together is Europe. What makes our lives easier somehow is Europe. What makes Europe's life more difficult, however, is that there is no shared story.

BIRKE HÄCKER

"Legal identity" in modern-day Europe is to be found on two different levels: on the one hand in the various national legal traditions, and on the other hand on the supra-national plane. Consistent with the European motto "united in diversity," the main criterion is not external demarcation, but internal integration.

JÖRN LEONHARD

We have to tolerate differences and not level them prematurely if we want to make progress towards a new European core.

PARAG KHANNA

Europeans must be more unified in their approach to Asia to avoid being divided by China and others in the areas of investment and human rights.

JÖRG ROCHOLL

China and Germany are mutually interdependent. Germany and Europe need to develop strategically to be prepared for the challenges of the future.

GABRIEL FELBERMAYR

In a world of new geostrategic rivalry and systems competition, where key players are driven by zero-sum reasoning, Europe must ask itself what its own interests are and how it can defend them.

KAI A. KONRAD

In a world where a hegemonic power defines the goals of the alliance and these goals no longer correspond with the goals of the other members, the other members may focus on their own goals and pursue them independently.

TIMO MEYNHARDT

The European idea can strengthen the self-image of European leaders by offering strength and confidence.

HANS ULRICH OBRIST

There are many categories of the unbuilt. There are projects that are too big to be realized. There are also projects that are too small to be realized. There are projects that are censored, and then, as Doris Lessing once told me, there are projects that are self-censored. I think we all have projects that we have not yet dared to do.

STEFAN KORIOTH

The issue must be how the great project of European integration based on peace and liberty can gain new impetus and consent. A promising way forward could be the reduction of European responsibilities and a greater openness to particular issues that are not flattened by the horizontal effect of European law.

CORINNE MICHAELA FLICK

We should spend more time thinking about what constitutes Europe culturally, and then create rituals that help Europe to be united. The European idea needs emotion, and European citizens must be able to feel enthusiastic about it, as only then will a common feeling of European identity emerge.

SVEN SIMON

It is our decision whether to overcome old myths and meet current challenges. It is our decision whether to make the European Union sustainable through its economic, environmental, and security policy, and whether we Europeans altogether are able to act. The future of Europe is in our hands.

FREDRIK ERIXON

Unless Europe can establish itself in the vanguard of the market rules and institutions that will guide the 21st-century economy, it will find that the rest of the world will become less interested in Europe's position and contributions in other areas.

ROBERTO VIOLA

If Europe changes gear and starts looking at public services and the economy at large, and how to transform them digitally, we can create our own digital path, differentiating us from the "digital imperialism" approach of some, or the major influence of a few powerful players from the private sector.

MATTHIAS KARL

A truly legitimate competition policy can no longer ignore the question of how, in a system of undistorted competition, one should define relevant product and geographic markets.

RUPPRECHT PODSZUN

It is a misperception to see the absence of formal regulation as freedom. If there is no framework, rules are set by the strongest actors.

YAEL TAMIR

Acknowledging the way elites, maybe unintentionally, betrayed some of their duties to their people, we must ask ourselves how we are going to contribute to a process that allows more people to share in the opportunities we promised they will have. It is a challenge. If we meet this challenge, maybe we will be able to create a better political future for all of us.

CLAUDIA WIESNER

The EU combines economic prosperity and social equality with the values derived from Article 2 of the EU Treaty: respect for human dignity, freedom, democracy, equality, the rule of law, respect for human rights, pluralism, non-discrimination, tolerance, justice, solidarity, and the equality of women and men. This "European success model" is unparalleled in the world.

CHAPTER 1

EUROPE: IDEAS OF UNITY AND A SENSE OF CRISIS

JÖRN LEONHARD

What is Europe? What challenges does it face? And how can it exist in a world that is dominated by new competitors and the loss of many traditional certainties? Historically, Europe started out as a myth before becoming a rather vague geographical concept, and ultimately an actual space of experience. As a narrative, Europe first emerged from a myth that tells the famous tale of how Zeus/Jupiter transformed himself into a bull to carry off Europa. This was followed by many major reinterpretations that were always linked to the question of what Europe is and might be. To this day, these questions have lost none of their explosive power.

At the end of a crisis-filled 16th century, the century of the Reformation and the wars of religion, the rulers of the Habsburg dynasty imagined Europe as a queen, a virgin whose heart belonged to the Habsburg ancestral homeland, whose head lay in Spain, and who was expected to unite Europe all the way down to Sicily. The leitmotif of this idea was a Catholic universal monarchy, combined with high hopes of securing or restoring the unity of Christendom as the unity of the West. But the Reformation, the wars of religion, and subsequent religious civil wars took precedence over these ideas, and it was actually these experiences of violence, for example during the Thirty Years' War, that defined a crisis with far-reaching consequences.

From the 18th century onwards, people began to envision Europe as a map of languages. The philosophy of the Enlightenment, cultural self-discovery through literature, the juxtaposition of individual countries' own national cultures seemed to be developing into the basis of a European form of societalization. However, the experience of the French Revolution and the Napoleonic regime gave rise to completely different ideas: at the height of Napoleon's domination of the continent and the establishment of the

Confederation of the Rhine, France held hegemonic sway over Europe. This was reflected in Napoleon's self-stylization as the successor to Charlemagne. At the same time, this provoked national resistance movements, which in many places turned into the origins of later nationalist movements. In addressing these aspirations, the 19th century developed into a period of national wars, for example in the Italian Risorgimento, which went on until 1859/61, or in the wars of 1864, 1866, and 1870/71, which created a "Lesser German" nation state under Prussian rule. For people living in the 1860s, Europe seemed at times to be a pawn in the struggle between war and peace.

However, pre-1914 Europe was much more than the mere sum of nation states and continental European empires, i.e. the Russian Tsarist Empire, the Habsburg monarchy, and the Ottoman Empire. Already before 1914, it also symbolized a kind of globalization before globalization, whose influence reached far beyond the territorial borders of European states and empires. The global network of telegraph lines before 1914, with its distinctive "highways of empire," echoed the routes of modern communications and media society, where Europe still played an important role as one of the centers of the world alongside the Americas and Asia. At the same time, given that most European countries were monarchies, there was still hope that European dynasts and monarchs would ultimately succeed in preventing the outbreak of a major war. This Europe of dynasties, of centuries-old European princely families with their personal connections, would undergo a profound upheaval during and after World War I. In an age of ideological extremes, these experiences gave rise to completely different ideas about Europe, for example in the shape of National Socialism, whose propagandists conceived Europe's historic mission as a radical war of extermination against Bolshevism and the Jews, based on German hegemony over continental Europe.

The climax of this phase and the transformation into completely different models of European societalization after 1945 were signaled by the turning point of World War II. In September 1942 Germany's National Socialist regime and Japan's expansion into Asia and the Pacific reached their widest territorial expansion. From this moment on, a gradual erosion set in, which, after the dual defeat of Germany and Japan in 1945, enabled Europe to take on a completely different role over the long term. At the end of World War II a bipolar structure emerged in the shape of the Cold War. In Western Europe, which was not part of the bloc dominated by the Soviet Union, an arduous path towards the first attempts at integration was emerging. After the first tentative efforts in the wake of the peace treaties of 1919, it is no coincidence that they concentrated on the communitization and internationalization of key industries. As young men, the founding fathers of the European Union Robert Schuman and Jean Monnet had watched with interest as the new world order was created at the 1919 Paris Peace Conference. After 1945 it became even more important to find a way out of the highly emotional spiral of negativity, out of the permanent distrust that existed between Germany and France in particular. Although initial ideas about forming Franco-German supervisory boards in large companies, for example, had already been developed soon after 1918, it was only possible to realize such concepts after World War II in the form of the European Coal and Steel Union. Such economic and political integration formed the basis for the gradual process of political communitization. In 1973, and after the launch of the Common Market, people at that time wondered what the aim of further European integration beyond the economic rationale might be. Since then, an emotional, affective void has opened up—namely the question of which values Europe should embody beyond the rationality of the economic market.

If we look at Europe's recent history from a historical point of view, ideas of unity and a sense of crisis always go together. Against this background, we might think of Europe in terms of "axial ages." In 1949 the German philosopher Karl Jaspers argued that the period between 800 and 200 BCE was a global cultural axial age, when the Judeo-Christian tradition, Buddhism, and Islam emerged—as well as, ultimately, all the important ideas and currents of Greek philosophy. In this axial age, Jaspers writes, the secular and the divine moved apart, with the result that the god-kings and gods, who had previously been perceived as existing in the world, were no longer conceivable. This launched a development that was to be crucial for Europe, namely that political power could become the object of criticism and could be held up against superior standards.

In the transition from antiquity to the Middle Ages, when the Roman Empire split in two and Europe was imagined in more territorial form for the first time, this division created a dual tension between Western and Byzantine Christianity and Church structure, and between Christianity and Islam—tensions that persist today. Both are fundamental in the history of Russia and the Ottoman Empire, as well as of modern Turkey.

In the Middle Ages, as we have already seen, a new idea of European unity emerged, based on the notion of a Christian West and a universal monarchy. These circumstances gave rise not least to the persona of Charlemagne, as well as to self-perceptions within the Holy Roman Empire of the German Nation, whose representatives invoked this tradition and the continuity of empires. It was only in the 18th-century Enlightenment that a deeper sense of a special historical path for Europe would emerge for the first time. Europe appeared as an expression of history's potential for development, of historical progress, and of a special kind of modernity, on which the civilization of the whole world would necessarily be based. From this perspective, Jaspers' "axial age" links to Reinhart Koselleck's notion of *Sattelzeit* [saddle period], during which, between 1770 and 1830, the modern vocabulary of politics and society developed—the modern "isms" of liberalism, socialism, communism, modern conservatism, as well as the concepts of nation and nationalism. From about the same time, in the 1860s at the latest, a particular sense of crisis emerged, as represented by Friedrich Nietzsche's cultural criticism or Max Weber's sociological investigations of his own era. Drawing on their own contemporary experiences, both pointed to a crisis in Europe's special path, for example when Max Weber asked what were the distinguishing characteristics of the Orient and the Occident. This latent crisis came to a head in the outbreak of World War I, in the revolutions and counter-revolutions that took place between 1917 and 1923, and in the strains on postwar societies.

The upheaval of the two world wars ushered in an intensified examination of the dichotomy-based model of center and periphery, of Europe and the world beyond its borders. Since the 1840s, the French historian and writer Alexis de Tocqueville had been asking whether modern democracy was no longer evolving in Europe, but rather in the United States. The proliferation of global centers and the multiple modernities associated with them was also a 19th-century inheritance. It is part of the prehistory of the bipolarity in which Europe looks to the United States on the one hand and to China on the other—a situation that still preoccupies us today.

So what might be defined as specific to Europe? There are, above all, six particular historical experiences of crisis that have shaped European history since the Early Modern period. At the same time, in these crisis experiences we can identify the stimuli for innovation that have characterized Europe again and again.

First, in the trauma of the religious civil wars of the 16th and 17th centuries, the unity of faith and the idea of a unifying, homogeneous West both collapsed. But at the same time, these civil wars formed the starting point for a new way of dealing with religious diversity. The history of modern tolerance, the modern concept of sovereignty and international law, and the history of the relationship between Church and State is inconceivable without these experiences, long before the Enlightenment.

Second, in the early 18th century a new kind of differentiation between the public and private realms emerged, which would shape the notion of individual autonomy as decisively as did the culture of law as a regulatory idea.

Third, at the end of the 18th century, two revolutions broke out in the American colonies and in France. They were shaped not only by the political and constitutional sphere, linked to constitutions, the rule of law, and parliaments, but also to a social and economic dynamic that could be identified in Great Britain as early industrialization. History seemed to be malleable; it was no longer immutable fate, and it presupposed a future that was open. Reinhart Koselleck has described this using the concept of "surplus expectations" and has explained how modern "isms" arose from such experiences of surplus, from a future that was anticipated and could be foreseen. This context produced new responses to the polarization of state and society that had been experienced in the revolutions since 1776 and 1789—not only the violent aspects of revolution, but also its reforms and the possibility of institutionalized compromise. All of this is part of the history of the impact of these revolutions. At the same time, as an expression of this particularly distinctive ambivalence, the problem of democratization emerged as a dual tension between freedom and equality and between freedom and security. Many of today's debates about the relationship between social inequality and political freedom or between personal freedom and vigilance in the age of digitalization are based fundamentally on these developments.

Fourth, as a result of industrialization and demographic change, specific social and political conflicts concerning integration developed. The range of social classes within Europe demanded new responses to the relationship between capital and labor, for example in the form of trade unions, the idea of cooperative societies, the concept of the welfare state, and debates about the limits of the market—a process that continues today and that was largely nourished by 19th-century experiences in Europe.

Fifth, in light of the new concept of sovereignty of the people, the revolutions gave rise to nations and nation states, while old empires, the Habsburg monarchy, the Russian Tsarist empire, and the Ottoman empire were called into question by these new nation states. This development was linked to the ideal of the internal homogenization of states and societies, and to the growth of the state in the era of compulsory education, taxation, conscription, and the right to vote, and this was still based on experiences of war. But since the late 19th and early 20th centuries, important new approaches resulted from this experience of war and violence, such as the idea of a variable and flexible balance of powers to prevent efforts to achieve hegemony, the concept of modern international law, and lastly, after 1918, the idea of collective security, for example in the League of Nations and, in the long term, the United Nations. Ultimately, the European nation state of the 19th century also acted as a repository of democracy and the possibility of social mobility, of the right to vote and compulsory education, but also of compulsory military service—here too it is impossible to ignore the ambivalence of Europe, in its juxtaposition of the promise of participation and violence.

Sixth, a key feature of Europe is the story of how it grew and expanded beyond its borders before ultimately shrinking as a result of decolonization. All nation states in Europe became empire-building nation states over the course of the 19th century. In 1914 Belgium had a colonial empire that was more than 20 times larger than Belgium itself. This imperial expansion, combined with increasing international competition, also led to the Balkan Wars of the early 20th century and these experiences fueled attempts at economic and later political integration after 1945. Thus, after 1945 and in light of the end of the European colonial regimes in Asia and Africa, European integration could become more dynamic—with Franco-German reconciliation continuously emphasized at its heart since the beginning of the 1960s. This connection can be seen in the fact that the Franco-German Élysée Treaty was concluded just one year after the Évian Accords, in which France granted Algeria independence in 1962.

But a closer look also shows how difficult it is to formulate a concise self-image for the present-day out of such points of reference. There is controversy over what ultimately constitutes Europe, and on what basis Europe should assert itself in the future. And maybe there is something productive in this debate, because it is only in this way that the achievements and risks become tangible.

A powerful narrative of peace emerged from the ongoing success story of 70 years of peace created by European integration. After the world wars, Europe became a realm of peace like no other in modern history. This peacekeeping role was very successful on three occasions: after 1945, in leading West Germany politically, economically, and mentally out of the catastrophe of National Socialism and the isolation of the postwar period; in the reintegration of authoritarian states and societies such as Greece, Spain, and Portugal since the 1970s; and again after the end of the Cold War in 1989/90 through the eastward expansion of the European Union. However, the concept of Europe as a "benevolent empire" that is incapable of a war of aggression and successfully keeps the peace on its borders is now reaching its limits, whether in former Yugoslavia in the 1990s, today in Eastern Ukraine, the Near and Middle East, or in North Africa. As rich as the story we have outlined here may be, it is no guarantee that Europe is capable of permanent self-renewal.

The path from Europe in around 1500, a patchwork territory of over 400 sovereign entities, via the long road to the Maastricht Treaty was time and again marked by incisive reallocations of lands that repeatedly went hand in hand with war and violence, whether between 1792 and 1815 or after 1918 and after 1945. But this is a story of waves of innovation and learning processes just as much as of ambivalences and problematic legacies. Throughout its history, Europe has been an ambiguous entity that cannot be determined by territorial unity but rather by experiences of conflict and a permanent engagement with political, social, and economic models and cultural interpretations.

That is why it is so fundamentally important to understand the historical differences behind the rhetoric of integration, and not smooth them out. For example, France became a nation state with defined borders at a relatively early stage, while Poland lost its statehood at the end of the 18th century, did not regain it until after 1918—and only won full sovereignty again after the end of the Cold War in 1989/91. This explains the many reservations about an excessive transfer of sovereignty rights in the context of the European Union. The legacy of diversity is also evident on other levels, as Europe contains at least three legal traditions in the forms of Roman and Germanic law as well as English common law. How on earth can a common European legal culture be created from this? We have to tolerate these differences and not level them prematurely if we want to make progress towards a new European core.

There has always been a particular connection between the experience of crises and the debate about the value of Europe. For example, it was no accident that the question of a European identity intensified during the 1970s, when the economic boom was subsiding and the oil crisis revealed the vulnerability of the economy. While European integration facilitated the peaceful end of the Cold War in 1989, since then global conflicts have jeopardized Europe's historical peace project. This became apparent after the outbreak of the financial crisis in 2008 and the intensification of foreign policy crises since 2014—from Russia's annexation of Crimea and the "Cold Peace" between the United States and Russia, via the refugee crisis and its many social consequences, to the crisis year of 2016 with the Brexit referendum and the election of Donald Trump, which accelerated the end of the era of the United States as Europe's protective power. This development is interwoven with the rise of China to the status of a global economic power. The underlying question is whether an authoritarian state economy based on one-party rule and the extensive control of individual rights is ultimately superior to the liberal, democratic model and a form of capitalism that is contained by society.

Will Europe remain stuck in a form of strategic defensiveness that it cannot currently transcend? Despite all the criticism, Europe's potential for innovation based on a liberal system, its importance as an economic market, and its achievement as the most successful modern-day peace project offer ways of building a positive narrative with which people can identify. It is no coincidence that so many people from the world's crisis regions are still risking their lives to reach this kind of Europe.

References

Lorraine Bluche, Veronika Lipphardt, and Kiran Klaus Patel (eds.), *Der Europäer – ein Konstrukt. Wissensbestände, Diskurse, Praktiken* (Göttingen: Wallstein Verlag, 2009).

Norman Davies, *Europe. A History* (Oxford: Oxford University Press, 1996).

Hans Joas and Klaus Wiegandt (eds.), *The Cultural Values of Europe*, trans. Alex Skinner (Liverpool: Liverpool University Press, 2008).

Tony Judt, *Postwar. A History of Europe Since 1945* (New York: Vintage, 2005).

Ferdinand Seibt, *Die Begründung Europas. Ein Zwischenbericht über die letzten tausend Jahre* (Frankfurt am Main: Fischer, 2002).

Wolfgang Schmale, *Geschichte Europas* (Vienna: Böhlau, 2000).

Bernd Schneidmüller, *Grenzerfahrung und monarchische Ordnung: Europa 1200–1500* (Munich: C.H. Beck, 2011).

Gerhard Schulz, *Europa und der Globus. Staaten und Imperien seit dem Altertum* (Stuttgart: DVA, 2001).

Brendan Simms, *Europe: The Struggle for Supremacy 1453 to the Present* (London: Allen Lane, 2014).

Willibald Steinmetz, *Europa im 19. Jahrhundert* (Frankfurt am Main: Fischer, 2019).

Andreas Wirsching, *Der Preis der Freiheit. Geschichte Europas in unserer Zeit* (Munich: C.H. Beck, 2012).

CHAPTER 2

EUROPEAN LEGAL IDENTITIES AND EUROPEAN LEGAL IDENTITY

BIRKE HÄCKER

If there is such a thing as a "law of the world," then it is in large parts European, at least in origin. Globally, the three biggest "legal families"—as comparative scholarship calls them—have their historical roots and their respective "mother legal orders" or "lead systems" in Europe. These are the French legal system for the so-called "Romance" or "Romanistic" legal family, German-speaking systems (i.e. German, Austrian, and Swiss law) for the "Germanic" legal family, and English law for the "Anglo-American" or "common law" family.[1] The former two are both founded on the tradition of Roman and canon law (mediated via the so-called *ius commune*, the "common" law of Continental Europe as it became established in the late medieval and Early Modern period), while English common law developed by and large independently of these influences (as a result of England undergoing centralization relatively early in political and administrative terms following the Norman Conquest).

For centuries, the legal material that sprang from these European sources was exported all over the world, particularly during the colonial era. Sometimes it would also be very deliberately imported by "enlightened" local rulers for political or economic reasons, and occasionally it was simply "transplanted" into a wholly different society.[2] Within numerous different countries, the material subsequently evolved further under local conditions; what emerged was often a unique mix of various traditions. This accounts for the fact that large parts of Latin America are to this day strongly influenced by the French *Code civil* (or *Code Napoléon* of 1804). Japan has a civil code whose structure resembles the German civil code (*Bürgerliches Gesetzbuch* or BGB of 1896), but whose content owes just as much to the French *Code civil*. It may further surprise the reader to learn that Turkish private law is modeled on the Swiss example or that South Africa operates a mixed system combining the Roman–Dutch law that the first Dutch settlers had brought with them and elements of the English common law. Within the Anglo-American legal family, due to the relatively early political independence of the United States, there developed a marked distinction between US American law on the one hand and, on the other, the group of common-law systems that are still much more closely related to English law (including Australian, New Zealand, or Singaporean law).

Of course the law of different countries draws not merely on European material, but also on a whole series of other sources, such as religious precepts or customs passed down orally from generation to generation. Yet in light of the global picture outlined above it is hard to escape the question of whether there is such a thing as a specific "European legal identity" and, if so, what lies at its core. This question, it is submitted, needs to be tackled on two levels, perhaps best reflected in the European Union's official motto "united in diversity" (*in varietate concordia*). First, it indicates that we ought to uncover and appreciate the rich diversity of the various strands of legal tradition from which today's national legal orders within Europe have sprung. Second, it suggests the existence of a supranational consensus on certain key issues uniting European states and citizens and thereby potentially bestowing on them a shared European legal identity.

EUROPEAN LEGAL IDENTITIES AT THE NATIONAL LEVEL

Looking at the national level, one finds Europe boasting a truly remarkable degree of legal diversity. Individual states (or groups of states)[3] each have their own historically grown features and distinctive characteristics. The contrasts between them are manifold and often substantial; in certain respects they are indeed so great that they generate real tensions between the systems—which of course also paves the way for regulatory competition and mutual inspiration. It is impossible within the confines of this essay to trace the whole complex panorama even in broad outline, so the present discussion will restrict itself to a few examples taken from the three "lead systems" mentioned above, namely French, English, and German law.

For one, the basic tenor of the English common law with its distinct mercantile flavor differs significantly from the Continental European codifications that have been enacted since the late 18th century. As already indicated by their name, "civil codes" such as the

French or German are geared towards the paradigm of a civil society. They establish the legal framework within which free and equal *citizens* meet, interact, and pursue their private aims. They are supplemented by a series of commercial codes containing additional or special legal rules for merchants and businesses. By contrast, English law, which has always resisted calls for a comprehensive codification and which therefore still flows primarily from judge-made precedents, continues to reflect (of necessity) the aspirations and values of its commercial classes. Their international trade connections, and their willingness—and financial ability—to take disputes to court where required, fundamentally shaped the legal landscape in England. By the 18th century, English law had fully absorbed the European Law Merchant (*lex mercatoria*), a system of trade practices and rules which had been developed since medieval times to cater for cross-border commercial transactions. Barry Nicholas, formerly Professor of Comparative Law at the University of Oxford, once explained the contrast as follows:

> There is...an important difference of emphasis between the Common law and the Civil law. Any generalisation is an exaggeration, but I think that one can venture to say this. The philosophy of the Common law is utilitarian and its primary concern is

with the economic exchange between the parties. The philosophy of the Civil law, it has been said, is closer to that of Kant. It is primarily concerned, not with the economic exchange between the parties, but with the exchange of consents and with the moral evaluation of the behaviour of the parties. This difference reflects differences in the histories of the two systems – the influence of Canon law on the Civil law and of commercial practice on the Common law. A consequence of this commercial orientation of the Common law is that if a choice has to be made between certainty and justice in the individual case, it is likely to be made in favour of certainty.[4]

It is indeed possible to regard the English common law as embodying the ethos of Hobbes, Lock, and Bentham, with the French *Code civil* reflecting the enlightened philosophy of Voltaire and Rousseau, and the German BGB having absorbed some of the spirit of the German Idealist tradition (one can debate how much of Kant and how much of Hegel).[5] Certain differences are already evident in the way in which the societal function of law is perceived on both sides of the Channel: to the English mind, the law provides a framework within which individuals can act and arrange their affairs without intervention by the state (negative conception of liberty). According to French and German thinking, by contrast, the law is essential in *enabling* individuals to realize their private autonomy; it is freedom *through* law (positive conception of liberty). This may be one of the reasons which English lawyers like to characterize—or rather caricature—the distinction between the two legal traditions by claiming that, under the common-law regime, everything is allowed which is not expressly forbidden, while in civilian systems everything is forbidden unless expressly authorized by the law.

The different perceptions of the relationship between the individual and the state are even further reaching than this. In continental legal thinking, there developed since the French Revolution a clear demarcation line between "private" law and "public" (i.e. constitutional as well as administrative) law, manifesting itself both in substantive and in procedural terms. Public law disputes between individual citizens and public authorities are typically assigned to specialized administrative courts to be decided in accordance with specific principles of administrative law and procedure, while private law disputes are allocated to the ordinary courts and governed by ordinary private law principles. In England, by contrast, the starting point is a single body of law, to be applied and continuously developed further by the ordinary courts. According to Albert Venn Dicey, whose seminal treatise recorded the principles of the unwritten British constitution at the end of the 19th century, this was to the English mind a fundamental aspect of the rule of law:

> [E]very man, whatever be his rank or condition, is subject to the ordinary law of the realm and amenable to the jurisdiction of the ordinary tribunals. In England the idea of legal equality, or of the universal subjection of all classes to one law administered by the ordinary Courts, has been pushed to its utmost limit. With us every official, from the Prime Minister down to a constable or a collector of taxes, is under the same responsibility for every act done without justification as any other citizen.[6]

Yet legal diversity within Europe is by no means confined to the juxtaposition of common law and civil law, as will be immediately evident from a simple comparison between the French and German legal orders. For one, the style of their respective private-law codifications differs. While the *Code civil* of 1804 is drafted in a simple, elegant language, deliberately chosen to be accessible to the lay person (something for which Napoleon Bonaparte himself is reputed to have pushed), the BGB of 1896 is a highly complex, technical, and precise product of German 19th-century private-law scholarship, addressed to a specialized cast of legal experts, but hardly comprehensible to lay readers. Its technical and sober style also lacks the slightly moralizing tendencies of the *Code civil*. The contrast between the two legal systems may have increased further since World War II under the influence of the infamous French *dirigisme*. This has left its traces on the entire state order. As far as private law is concerned, the regime of extra-contractual (tortious) liability has become an extremely flexible tool of social policy of which French courts are making copious use. Leaving aside the philosophical background for the moment and concentrating on the *actual* regulatory function private law plays within civil society, and particularly the judicial role in all this, one is driven to conclude that the position of German law today is overall much closer to that of English law than to its immediate neighbor.

A necessary corollary of the great diversity among national legal systems is the opportunity for them to influence each other and to borrow from one another. The "fathers" (as they tend to be described) of the German BGB, for instance, routinely looked at and considered the way in which specific problems or conflicts of interests were resolved by existing private law codifications (such as in the French *Code civil* or by the Austrian General Code of Private Law [ABGB] of 1811) before deciding on the adoption or rejection of a proposed rule. Since the enactment of the BGB, many European systems have evolved their own "mix" of principles referable to different legal traditions and homegrown solutions. This is true, for example, of the Italian *Codice Civile* as redrafted in 1942, the Portuguese *Código Civil*, which was completely overhauled in 1966, and the *Nieuw Burgerlijk Wetboek* (New Dutch Civil Code) of 1992. Since about the middle of the 20th century, the English common law has also exerted a notable and, it seems, ever-increasing influence. The institution of the trust in particular has been an object of envy and emulation in Continental Europe due to its ability to function as a versatile and widely deployable vehicle for holding assets on a fiduciary basis. While the trust was initially imported only into the law of Liechtenstein (back in the 1920s), it is today recognized by a growing number of Eastern European states,[7] and both Luxembourg and France have attempted to create a functionally equivalent instrument in the form of a type of contract known as *fiducie*.[8] Speaking more generally, many a continental legislator is looking with covetous eyes at the popularity among the international business community of English law as a law of choice and of London as a forum for litigation. This has been the impetus for numerous reforms in recent years—be it in the realm of substantive law or procedure, including the creation of English-speaking commercial courts in Paris, Frankfurt am Main, Hamburg, and Amsterdam—all driven by the idea of there being a "market for law" and a degree of beneficial "regulatory competition" between European states.[9]

A SUPRANATIONAL EUROPEAN LEGAL IDENTITY?

Turning to the question of whether there is, amid all this legal diversity, a trans- or supranational legal identity connecting the various European states and at the same time setting them apart from the rest of the world, we can observe at the outset that it will hardly be possible to identify individual legal norms or institutions as being "exclusive" to Europe. As seen above, law of European origin is nowadays disseminated throughout the world, and European voices (both those purporting to speak for the continent as a whole and those emanating from individual legal systems) are constantly participating in international legal discourse.

The most promising place to find a specifically "European" legal identity is therefore to be located in the fields in which European states have come together to create common structures at the supranational level: in the European Convention on Human Rights (ECHR) and—independently thereof, smaller, but politically more significant—within the framework of the European Union (EU), i.e. the former European Communities. Although the starting point of European integration was economic collaboration, and although economic intertwinement remains a key aspect, the European Court of Justice soon began to distil "general principles of law" from the "constitutional traditions common to the Member States" as well as the ECHR, thereby identifying and establishing a set of basic values shared by all.[10] This shared European legal culture is most distinct in the area of fundamental rights and the rule of law. It is surrounded and supplemented by various layers of positive EU rules and principles, developed into a whole body of law over the years (the so-called *acquis communautaire*), which also contributes towards creating a common identity. At its core lies a market-orientated and liberal economic constitution founded upon the four basic freedoms, coupled with a high level of consumer and environmental protection and sophisticated labor-law standards. After the fall of the Iron Curtain, it was reference to these two supranational role models, the Council of

Europe on the one hand and the European (Economic) Community on the other, that enabled many Eastern European states to re-imagine themselves in a new European mold within a relatively short period of time, thereby accelerating their integration into the existing community of "Western" states.

To the extent that integration under the aegis of the EU has resulted in the association of European Member States turning from a pure economic community into a political organization with a broad remit, the identity question also begins to arise for citizens of the constituent countries. From a supranational perspective, individuals are no longer mere actors within the Single Market but, since the Treaty of Maastricht, also citizens of the European Union. As such, they are endowed with personal rights and duties, including the freedom to choose their place of residence, forms of democratic participation (e.g. at local elections in the country of residence), and a well-defended claim to equal treatment. Yet this legal framework alone does not automatically guarantee that all Germans, Italians, French, Polish, Spanish, or Hungarian citizens will also feel and identify as "European." If any proof was required, the fact that a majority of UK citizens voted to leave the European Union in the 2016 Brexit referendum demonstrated that there is still a widespread emotional distance between the EU as a supranational association and the people of individual Member States. It is, we may conclude, not enough formally to postulate and to fill with life an idea of EU citizenship, so long as large parts of the population do not experience and acknowledge this status as part of their everyday reality.

That is precisely the starting point of attempts to establish and enhance, by legal means, a genuine European citizen identity. Traditionally, the selective assimilation of specific aspects of the law as between the Member States was understood as a mere instrument for the creation and facilitation of the European Single Market. However, historical experience shows that the unification (or at least far-reaching harmonization) of larger areas of the law, especially of private law, is capable is exerting a strong integrative force through provision of a common legal identity and reference point for individual members of a political community.[11] During the period in which the European nation states first evolved, monarchs and other governors already understood that codifications of the law could function as a powerful symbol of national unity, providing internal coherence while at the same time externally delimiting the state as one entity. The French *Code civil* exemplified this symbolism so successfully that the German political movement for national unity, which gained impetus in early 19th century, called for a parallel German civil code to be compiled, in order to further the cause of the desired unification.[12]

How fast, and in what form, common rules and principles could—and ought to—expedite the formation of a genuinely European civil society is nevertheless a matter of some debate. For a while it looked as though a comprehensive and detailed codification of substantial parts of core private law might be within reach. Ambitious academic projects such as the so-called *Draft Common Frame of Reference* had done a great deal of preliminary work within a comparatively short period of time, all with the approval and support of the European Parliament and the Commission,[13] and the political will appeared to be there to push (in due course) for a common European civil code, even in the face of significant opposition within the Member States. Yet when the Commission led by Jean-Claude Juncker took office at the end of 2014, a much more modest proposal for a Regulation on a Common European Sales Law,[14] which had already been through several rounds of fine-tuning, was withdrawn to the surprise of many. Even though the cause of legal unification within Europe has, as a result, lost some of its momentum, there remains the vision of using "soft harmonization" gradually to build a transnational civil society capable of sustaining the existing political institutions and providing them with greater legitimacy. Hugh Collins, for instance, has argued in this vein:

> My argument is that the European Union needs a civil code, not for completing the Single Market but as a vital contribution to the building of a cosmopolitan polis that will enable the Union to achieve its praiseworthy goals in cooperation with the Member States. In a multilevel system of governance, where powers are shared between national and federal elements of government, without a unified court structure, the civil code must be a code of principles that provide a gravitational pull towards harmonization rather than attempt through detailed rules to impose uniformity. These principles contained in the civil code can draw upon the cosmopolitan traditions of private law, through which legal scholars have developed legal doctrine by borrowing from tradition, comparison between legal systems, and philosophical reflection. But on its own the cosmopolitan tradition that reveals a common core of principles is insufficient, for the European civil code needs to harmonize its provisions with European social model and the contemporary aspirations of its citizens to social justice.[15]

The tricky issue here is always striking the right balance between imposing a fast, but potentially forced and artificial "top down" assimilation of the law, and fostering a slower, organic, "bottom up" convergence. Such a "bottom up" convergence can only be achieved through the rediscovery and the intensive study and debate of the shared historic roots out of which the different European legal traditions have grown. It is the search for a "new European *ius commune*," founded not only upon continental heritage, but also including the English common law.[16] It is true that it might, *prima facie*, be easier to leave English law to one side and concentrate on finding a common denominator for the civil law systems which are all more firmly grounded in the Roman and canon tradition. However, the strong gravitational pull and inspirational force which the common law has exerted over the past decades indicates that—quite irrespective of the United Kingdom's departure from the EU—it is neither feasible nor advisable to establish a supranational European legal identity without recourse to the common law's values and institutions (not least because Irish law is based on English law and Ireland will continue to participate fully in the process of European integration). The common law is an essential component of Europe's rich national diversity, whose wealth of ideas and solutions provides the cradle of and accounts for the special potential of legal assimilation within Europe.

The *leitmotiv* "united in diversity" is hence also a suitable motto for the complex interplay of national legal identities at Member State level with the evolving supranational legal order and its identity-generating characteristics on the European plane. The latter cannot be defined primarily as something through which Europe sets itself apart from the rest of the world. Instead, what is at issue is the constructive entanglement and/or merger of various strands of grown traditions, each of which European states share with many countries around the world. It is precisely this margin of variation and its ability to connect up in manifold ways within the parameters of a larger framework that accounts for Europe's unique legal identity.

Notes

1. For details see Konrad Zweigert and Hein Kötz, *An Introduction to Comparative Law*, trans. Tony Weir, 3rd edn. (Oxford: Oxford University Press, 1998) ch. 5 *et seq.*

2. This metaphor is most closely associated with Alan Watson, *Legal Transplants: An Approach to Comparative Law* (Edinburgh: Scottish Academic Press, 1974).

3. Beside the "Romance/Romanistic" legal family (consisting mainly of France, Belgium, Luxembourg, Italy, and Spain),

the "Germanic" legal family (consisting mainly of Germany, Austria, Switzerland, Greece, and Turkey) and the common-law family (consisting mainly of England, Wales, and Ireland), the Scandinavian countries (i.e. Denmark, Sweden, Norway, Finland, and Iceland) are often described as a separate, but internally coherent group of jurisdictions making up the "Nordic" legal family.

4. Barry Nicholas, "The United Kingdom and the Vienna Sales Convention: Another Case of Splendid Isolation?" (Rome: Centro di studi e ricerche di diritto comparato e straniero, 2003), https://www.cisg.law.pace.edu/cisg/biblio/nicholas3.html (accessed 17 November 17, 2019).

5. See Knut Wolfgang Nörr, *Eher Hegel als Kant: Zum Privatrechtsverständnis im 19. Jahrhundert* (Paderborn: Ferdinand Schöningh, 1991).

6. Albert Venn Dicey, *Introduction to the Study of the Law of the Constitution*, 3rd edn. (London: Macmillan & Co, 1889), p. 181.

7. Most notably in Hungary and the Czech Republic.

8. See, for instance, Art. 2011 *et seq.* of the French *Code civil* (in existence since 2007).

9. Critical: Johanna Stark, *Law for Sale: A Philosophical Critique of Regulatory Competition* (Oxford: Oxford University Press, 2019).

10. Fundamental in this respect: ECJ, Judgment of December 17, 1970, Case 11/70, [1970] ECR 1125, esp. para. 4 (*Internationale Handelsgesellschaft*); Judgment of May 14, 1974, Case 4/73, [1974] ECR 491, esp. para. 13 (*Nold*); judgment of October 28, 1975, Case 36/75, [1975] ECR 1219, esp. para. 32 (*Rutili*); Judgment of December 13, 1979, Case 44/79, [1979] ECR 3727, esp. paras. 15, 17–18 (*Hauer*).

11. Cf. the differentiated and ultimately sceptical discussion of these issues by Nils Jansen, *Binnenmarkt, Privatrecht und*

europäische Identität (Tübingen: Mohr Siebeck, 2004) who regards the 18th- and 19th-century idea of codification (see p. 19) as being tied to a "romantically exaggerated" vision of it functioning as a "symbol and expression of national identity" and who concludes (see p. 83) that a codification which truly promotes identity-building needs to be based on "genuine consensus" rather than "mere compromise."

12. In 1814 this led to the famous so-called "codification dispute" between Anton Friedrich Justus Thibaut and Friedrich Carl von Savigny.

13. Study Group on a European Civil Code and Research Group on the Existing EC Private Law (Acquis Group), *Principles, Definitions and Model Rules of European Private Law: Draft Common Frame of Reference (DCFR)* (Munich: Sellier European Law Publishers, 2009).

14. Proposal for a Regulation of the European Parliament and of the Council on a Common European Sales Law, COM/2011/0635 final – 2011/0284 (COD).

15. Hugh Collins, "Why Europe Needs a Civil Code" in (2013) *European Review of Private Law* vol. 21 (2013), pp. 907–922, here pp. 922–923 (footnote omitted).

16. Seminal in this respect: Reinhard Zimmermann, "Das römisch-kanonische ius commune als Grundlage europäischer Rechtseinheit" in *Juristenzeitung* 8 (1992), esp. pp. 15 *et seq.*

CHAPTER 3

WHERE IS EUROPE GOING? AN APPEAL FOR MORE DIVERSITY IN THE EUROPEAN UNION

STEFAN KORIOTH

At the dawn of the 2020s, the European Union is not in good shape. While in the past the European Union (or before its creation, the European Community) regularly emerged from crises stronger, now the centrifugal forces appear to be spinning out of control. There is agreement on the evidence of crisis, but opinions differ as to why this is so and what can be done about it. As the disintegration of Europe or even the dissolution of the Union cannot be considered a serious alternative to European cooperation, the issue must be how the great project of European integration based on peace and liberty can gain new impetus and consent.

I.

The causes of the crisis in the EU have grown perilously over the last 20 years. In a keynote speech in 2017, Commission President Juncker spoke of a "polycrisis." Since 2008, the financial and debt crisis has revealed a profound gulf between the states in the north and the south of the European Union, casting doubt on the EU's promise of prosperity, and destroying any hope for the foreseeable future that the Euro might become the currency of all Member States. Within the monetary union, there is a unified monetary and currency policy, but no budgetary policy that is managed and controlled supranationally. The refugee and asylum crisis has thrown long-familiar institutional weaknesses into sharp relief. Embodying the principle that the Member State first entered by an asylum seeker assumes responsibility for providing asylum, the "Dublin" regime was never practicable because of the burden it placed on the countries of Southern Europe, nor was it implemented as such. In turn, this demonstrated the weakness of EU law in terms of enforcement and reform, law that remains binding until it is improved. These failures of implementation once again find a parallel in the financial crisis. No one assumes that the EU's numerous budgetary requirements will be implemented by the Member States in the event of a worst-case scenario.

Another crisis situation, Brexit began with Britain's legitimate or at least debatable criticism of the way in which the European institutions functioned, the jurisdiction of the European Court of Justice, and the latter's far-reaching incursions into Members' self-determination. The fact that this criticism could not be adequately translated into a measured debate about reform either at European or national level, leading instead to an almost uncontrollable disaster for both parties, means the loss of an important Member. It also shows, unfortunately, that withdrawal is the only viable way of escaping Europe's undesirable developments and impositions. The right course would have been a Europe-wide debate about Britain's grievances. To this extent, irrespective of Britain's internal specificities and Europe's feelings of resentment, the United Kingdom is also a victim of the Union's weakness. Without Britain, the Union will find it even harder to bring its institutional problems under control, especially in the relationship between the Commission and the Parliament. And Brexit means ceding criticism of the EU to the forces of nationalism and radicalism.

All these problems are accompanied by an increasing fragility in the fundamental consensus about the importance of the democratic principle and constitutional guarantees. And this has taken place against the backdrop of new forms of nationalism, which are invoked against the Union directly, at least in terms of rhetoric and propaganda, in ways that have not been seen at any other time over the last 60 years. In the face of this, the Union appears helpless, and the only effective antidote it has come up with is to grant or deny subsidies.

We are thus faced with an unfortunate combination. As a problem-solving organization the Union is overloaded when it comes to the tasks assigned to it. But it is also overloaded in respect of Europe's accessibility over many years as the recipient of projected hopes and expectations. Finally, there is the external perspective. It is of course true that the Union is the world's most important single market, producing impressive achievements and dismantling all internal barriers to development. However, in the globalized world order the economic importance of Europe is waning, and important decision-making processes are taking place between America and East Asia. In foreign policy terms, as its representatives acknowledge, the Union is simply paralyzed. There is no common stance with regard to either the Arab world or other parts of the globe, while the side effects of distant conflicts, not just in Syria, present a danger to Europe. The previous formula, whereby a current crisis—such as the "empty chair" policy of the 1960s, the mismanagement of the agricultural market system (the "butter mountain") and the "Eurosclerosis" of the 1980s, before the Single European Act (1986)—lay at the root of the subsequent compromise, which in turn launched a subsequent reform debate, no longer seems to function.

II.

When considering suggested solutions, we should go back to the beginning. A key proposition in the project of European integration, which was begun post-1949 initially by six Western and Central European states and now comprises 27 states, is over 100 years old. When the catastrophe of World War I began in Europe in August 1914, British Foreign Secretary Sir Edward Grey said: "The lamps are going out all over Europe, we shall not see them lit again in our lifetime." European integration was a way of overcoming the alternating world wars and civil wars of the first half of the 20th century. It was the result of the determination that was ultimately reached to overcome a violent and hostile situation and create what is today enshrined in Article 3, (1) and (2) of the Treaty on European Union (as amended by the 2009 Treaty of Lisbon): "The Union's aim is to promote peace, its values, and the well-being of its peoples. The Union shall offer its citizens an area of freedom, security, and justice without internal frontiers, in which the free movement of persons is ensured in conjunction with appropriate measures with respect to external border controls, asylum, immigration, and the prevention and combating of crime." On fundamental values, Article 2 states: "The Union is founded on the values of respect for human dignity, freedom, democracy, equality, the rule of law, and respect for human rights, including the rights of persons belonging to minorities. These values are common to the Member States in a society in which pluralism, non-discrimination, tolerance, justice, solidarity, and equality between women and men prevail."

These are grand words and, strictly speaking, normative demands, not descriptions of fact. In effect, the steps towards economic integration, culminating in the creation of the single market in 1992, were not very controversial, and only difficult in the case of the many individual issues that had to be resolved. There was and is more complexity when it comes to the shared values that have been specifically evoked since the foundation of the European Union in 1993 and which played a role in the debate well before this. From the start, the Community, today's European Union, was a community of rights, not a community with a comprehensive founding myth common to all citizens, a myth that could create legitimacy and consent. In this context, referring to the experiences of the first half of the 20th century falls short of the mark. It is not enough to want to overcome something, and certainly not to have already overcome something, as right and necessary as this may be. What is needed is a foundation that points to the future. The Union, like every single society within it, is based on a tacit plebiscite that must be repeated and affirmed every single day. There is no doubt that much has been achieved along the way—we have only to compare the level of integration already achieved with what the founders of integration in the 1950s, such as Robert Schuman and Konrad Adenauer, thought possible. But where do we want to go? Is there a common goal? What can Europe be in the future?

III.

There are a number of suggestions as to how these questions may be answered. The most striking suggestion may well be that of French President Macron, who in 2017 summed up his ideas by saying that Europe should be "sovereign, united, and democratic," with the emphasis on sovereignty. This is a characteristic that has not really been attributed to the Union thus far, but rather to individual states. It is the ability to determine one's own political and social system internally, and to be outwardly independent and free from interference by other states. Thus, the French proposal gives a radical twist to the old demand for further integration. The Union should be able to do what states can currently do, that is ultimately become a state. This may well be unrealistic, however. Major areas of disagreement exist, not just when it comes to fundamental values and principles, such as in the areas of democracy and the rule of law, but also in terms of internal solidarity, which is indispensable in a sovereign entity and arises from the feeling of togetherness—solidarity between different regions, or solidarity between rich and poor through redistribution and social security. Any attempt to anchor such manifestations of solidarity in Europe encounters defensive reactions. This shows that it will be very difficult to establish a sovereign Europe over and above its Members. Moreover, the lack of belief in Europe-wide reciprocal obligations of solidarity is the strongest indication that even in the future there will not be a "unified, European citizenry" that "creates its own parliamentary controlled central sovereign power."[1] The German Federal Constitutional Court interprets and limits the Basic Law's authority to take part in the European Union accordingly: "Article 23.1 of the Basic Law like Article 24.1 of the Basic Law underlines that the Federal Republic of Germany takes part in the development of a European Union designed as an association of sovereign states (*Staatenverbund*) to which sovereign powers are transferred. The concept of *Verbund* covers a close long-term association of states which remain sovereign, a treaty-based association which exercises public authority, but whose fundamental order is subject to the decision-making power of the Member States and in which the peoples, i.e. the citizens, of the Member States, remain the subjects of democratic legitimation."[2]

By contrast with Macron's suggestion, we can look at managing the European crisis of legitimation using mechanisms within the existing framework. A number of instruments are already available for this purpose.

For individual issues, subgroups of Members with different requirements can be created—"multispeed Europe"—and there are adaptation and experimentation clauses through which states can implement different ideas. Directives also allow for national organizational options (Article 288 of the Treaty on the Functioning of the European Union: "A directive shall be binding, as to the result to be achieved, upon each Member State to which it is addressed, but shall leave to the national authorities the choice of form and methods.") Perhaps Europe's acceptability could be enhanced by allowing more internal European diversity, alongside strict adherence to the common primary legal framework. Such ideas were already being mooted at the end of the 1980s, following the entry into force of the Single European Act (1986), but before the foundation of the Union, which at that time was only a possibility on the horizon. In 1986, the German author Hans Magnus Enzensberger toured various European countries, not only those of the then Community, and made an interesting observation: "What else is Europe but a conglomeration of mistakes? Mistakes that are so diverse that they complement and balance one another. Taken separately, we're each unbearable in our own way."[3] It is not a competition to find the best solution, as we in Germany are familiar with as a (questionable) way of legitimizing diversity within a federal state (such as different school systems versus a unified school-leaving exam), but rather the positive acknowledgment of diversity, without the constant ulterior motive of having to overcome this diversity unconditionally. There is much to suggest that a sense of unease about the Union arises from the fact that in many areas it makes decisions that in the context of the nation state would be constitutional decisions. A "creeping constitutionalization" is emerging within the Union, which has not been the subject of groundwork and feedback in political debates and compromises.[4]

Similarly, the unity on which Europe is founded is less broad than often described. Of course, there is a "unity of origin"[5] in Europe, originating in Greek and Roman antiquity, Christianity, and Judaism. But what exactly does that mean to us today, beyond common traditions in science, religion, culture, and ways of doing business (which, of course, is quite a lot)? The unity of origin is as important as it is "trivial."[6] It should not be forgotten that since the Middle Ages there has been something else, namely connections and tensions between beliefs and values in Europe, between rules and projects. On the one hand there was a shared consciousness, but on the other hand competition existed between different European centers of power and culture as well as types of system. Until 1806, an empire existed in the middle of Europe that claimed to transcend nations, was diversely structured, and was unable to become a state. Alongside this, in northern and western Europe, however, there was the alternative political model of the nation state. Without Europe's diverse centers of power and types of system, and without competition between these centers, neither European democracy, its various legal cultures, nor competitive European markets could have developed. Might this be a promising way forward even today? Currently there is an argument for the reduction of European responsibilities and a greater openness to particular issues that are not flattened by the horizontal effect of European law. In this context, the general principle of non-discrimination (Article 18 of the Treaty on the Functioning of the European Union), which is understood, in particular in the decisions of the European Court of Justice, as a mandate for the comprehensive equal treatment of persons and situations, has a particularly leveling effect. Anything that does not meet with universal acceptance cannot be enforced by the constraints of European law over the long term. In any case, it is unacceptable to deprive Member States of their scope for taking action and reposition it at European level, where it then cannot be fulfilled through lack of agreement.

Ultimately—and this also limits the Union's operational framework—Europe is indeed not a state. The Member States are still "masters of the Treaties," determining the Union's character and areas of action. In this way, then, Europe's character at any one moment is also a mirror of the nature of national societies. What the Union is attributed with and criticized for has its origin in the Member States and must be processed there too. Democratic shortcomings, lack of implementation of EU law, even obstruction—these phenomena are of national origin, and only in the second instance can they make an appearance at European level or even be resolved. Only then can we really say: "The European Union is a motley entity. The national, cultural, and linguistic diversity of Europe is not an historical burden to be shaken off; rather it constitutes the richness of the old continent. Nationalism has brought this to the fore, dividing nations; the European Union builds on what unites it. It would be in the very best interests of its Members if the EU could speak with one voice not only in terms of trade policy and the single market, but also on the major issues of foreign and security policy."[7]

Notes

1. Heinrich August Winkler, "Ein Anspruch auf tönernen Füßen" in *Frankfurter Allgemeine Zeitung*, June 29, 2019.

2. BVerfG, Decision of June 30, 2009 (2 BvE 2/08 et al.), note 229 (Lisbon Treaty).

3. Hans Magnus Enzensberger, *Europe, Europe: Forays into a Continent*, trans. Martin Chalmers (London: Hutchinson Radius, 1989), p. 228.

4. This is the argument made by, for example, Dieter Grimm, *Europa ja – aber welches? Zur Verfassung der europäischen Demokratie* (Munich: C.H. Beck, 2016), p. 45 ff.

5. Hermann Lübbe, "Die europäische Supranationalität und das Christentum" in Hartmut Behr and Mathias Hildebrand (eds.), *Politik und Religion in der Europäischen Union* (Wiesbaden: Springer, 2006), pp. 481 ff.

6. Lübbe, "Die europäische Supranationalität," p. 481.

7. Winkler, "Ein Anspruch auf tönernen Füßen."

CHAPTER 4

WHY NATIONALISM—A EUROPEAN IDENTITY

YAEL TAMIR

We are struggling with the outcomes of a series of social and political transformations that took us by surprise. It is natural to expect continuity, yet history teaches us that we are always on the move. Our political and social reality is constantly changing. Oscillating back and forth, sometimes it reaches the extremes, often it stops halfway. When we reach an extreme, we tend to describe it as a crisis, an unprecedented state of affairs.

In 2018 we saw the end of a hundred years of an ideological journey that has known highs and lows, starting with the "war to end all wars," culminating in the "end of history," and ending with the re-emergence of nationalism, Brexit, and a wave of separatist demands. The losing ideologies of the 20th century are back, fighting for a position in the front row; the winning ones are on the defensive. If there is a lesson to be learned from the last hundred years, it is that nothing ends or begins as abruptly as it seems. Ideologies do not die out or disappear; they put on new garments, some makeup, and a smile and come back in a new guise. Ideological debates are, therefore, here to stay.

Aware of this historical perspective, I would like to offer a positive interpretation of the present state of affairs, arguing that it should be seen as an invitation for soul-searching, a collective reflection on where we have gone right, but mostly on where we have gone wrong, in order to offer a fresh view on where we should be going.

Analyzing nationalism, one is obliged to remember its alarming aspects and horrific consequences. Yet nationalism is not all bad. The marriage of nationalism and democracy created Europe and much of the modern world. Kings and queens did not derive their legitimacy from those they governed but from the divine. Modern democracies claim to be representing a people's desire for self-rule. Nationalism shaped these demands in terms of personal and national liberation and self-determination, giving Western democracies and the modern welfare state a self to rely on.

It is very easy to reduce explanations of the present crises to particular explanations: Hillary Clinton failed to be elected because Americans were not ready for a female president, or because she was part of the Washington elite. People voted for Brexit because they did not understand the question. Angela Merkel lost power because she was governing for too long. There is some truth in all these claims but I am trying to look beyond particular cases in a search of a pattern that can offer a more general explanation. There will always be exceptions. One may say "In my country things work differently," but I think there is common ground, and understanding its nature is necessary in order to offer new ways of thinking and new solutions.

In what follows I would like to offer five explanations for the emerging crisis in the West.[1] The first has to with the growing social and economic gaps. Nowadays, social gaps have become a major source of concern. But if you look at the data, you will see that the gaps have been growing since the 1980s. If we had looked at them more carefully earlier, we might have revised our analysis of the effects of globalization and, maybe, acted to balance the social and economic playing field.

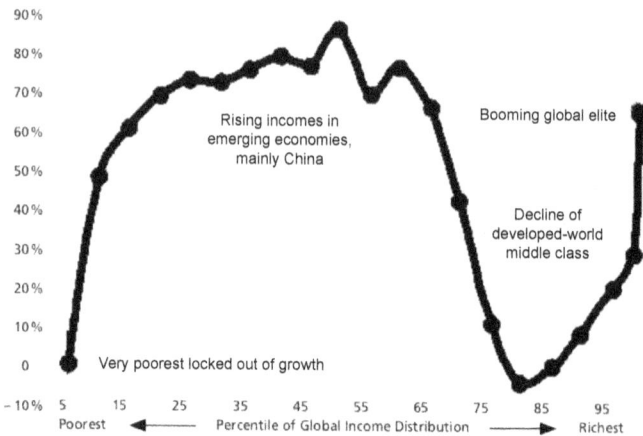

Global Income Growth 1988–2008

This graph, drawn up by an economist called Branko Milanović, illustrates the so-called "elephant curve."² It describes the pattern of global income growth between 2008 and 2018. What do we see? Globalization did raise the living standards of the poorest people in the poorest countries in the world. Sometimes it doubled their income. If you earned one dollar a day, now you earn two dollars a day, maybe even five. That is a major improvement. Now let us look at how things were getting worse for the middle classes in the West who are experiencing a constant decline in their living standards. On the other side of the graph—the "trunk

WHY NATIONALISM—A EUROPEAN IDENTITY

of the elephant"—lies the 10 percent, the global elite—and they are doing extremely well.

Since the 1980s, the middle classes have seen a decline in their ability to make a decent living, and consequently in their social status. For the first time in modern history, life expectancy in America is in decline. We never anticipated that the Western world would undergo such a period, and that decline in living standards would be a result of peace and prosperity rather than war.

The fading American Dream
Percentage of children earning more than their parents

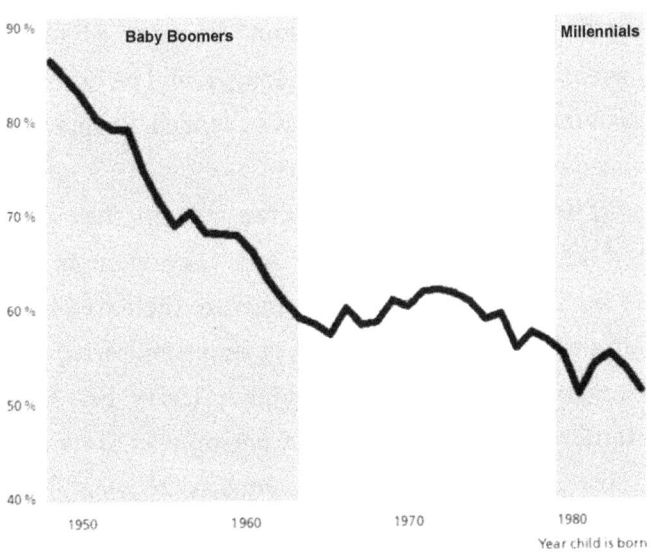

Source: The Equality of Opportunity Project

With the growing gaps comes another important factor: pessimism. If you examine the way people perceive their life, you will find that the middle classes in the West believe (and they are not wrong) that their children are going to be less well off than they are. A recent McKinsey report shows that in most of the OECD countries young people are going to be poorer than their parents, constantly struggling to make a living, buy a house, and pay back their loans.[3]

This is a massive transformation in the way people perceive the future. My parents were sure, and they were statistically right, that I will do better than them—that my generation would be more educated, have more opportunities, live longer, and be healthier than theirs. But now things have changed. People look ahead with anxiety.

It is important to remember that in the West, today's poor are better off than they were in the 1930s and 1940s. Yet people measure their wellbeing on a comparative basis. A very important article on equality by American philosopher Harry Frankfurt starts with a short dialogue. A person asks his friend: "How are your children?" "Compared to what?" the friend replies.[4] When they compare themselves to the well-off, today's poor feel their situation has gotten worse. The distance between them and the top 5 to 10 percent is incommensurable.

Feeling deprived is a good reason to rebel; feeling stuck is an even better one. Social mobility is on the decline, the traditional remedy—education—is working less well. We used to say to young people, "Your parents didn't have a high-school education; you have to go to college and you will do well." I grew up in a world that believed that education can fix everything: give people more education and they will be better off. But today we are in the most educated age ever, and the gaps are still growing. People who went to college and got a degree cannot find a job, and if they find a job, the job sometimes does not pay enough to make a living, and they have little chance of moving up the social ladder. This is a source of frustration for young people around the world, and frustrations breed unrest.

Unbeknown to most of us, a new class is emerging and growing: the educated poor. The educated poor are an unfulfilled class, because they have done everything right and they still cannot make a living. They cannot buy an apartment, and they do not know what the future of their children will be. All this leads to disillusionment. The assumptions that we are going to have an economy that keeps growing endlessly, prosperity is going to trickle down, and the middle class are going to get better, that everybody is going to get better, that this is a win-win situation, are all being questioned.

People are now questioning the paradigms that the liberal, progressive, global camp has been advocating for quite a long time. They are now saying: "This world order doesn't work for me, it doesn't work for my neighbor—who does it work for?" Hence, they ask themselves what they could do to change things for the better. People distrust the present political order partly because they feel that they cannot influence the way things are. A global sense of helplessness is spreading. Some call it a democratic deficit. One of the positive aspects of the present upheaval is that it proves that the present state of affairs is not immune to public pressure: people are taking to the streets in Singapore, Lebanon, and Spain. Their reasons for demonstrating are different but they are united by a feeling of optimism—they can bring about change. Democratically, this a very important development. If you cannot change anything, why play the game?

This is not to say that the leaders emerging out of this global crisis are democrats—often they are not. Yet the feeling that is spreading around that "we, the people, can make a difference" encourages people to become active political agents. We are therefore seeing people who have been feeling excluded from the political scene saying "We have power." The growing activism of dormant forces is a blessing, though it often comes with a price.

I am not claiming that things are changing in the right direction, but I am saying there is a great urge for change. Protesters are often labeled as populist, narrow-minded bigots, and there certainly are narrow-minded bigots among them, hateful people motivated by a misguided understanding of reality. Yet those who vote or protest against the system are telling us something important and true, something that leaders around the world should be attentive to.

This is why I am saying that, in a way, this crisis is a victory of the people who were silenced. They were abused by the elites, they were abused by international corporations, and by other global forces. These people are now saying "Enough!" Maybe the most important political duty today is to listen to these new forces entering the political arena, to hear the people who are crying out for change. Their complaints are important ones, as they touch the most basic things people care about: their children, their health, their work, their pension, their status, and their self-esteem. I urge us not to think of them as irrational, as people who misunderstand their position, but as people facing a real crisis.

One of the things that induced me to think about these new developments is looking at election maps. Election maps around the world share certain similarities. The mega-cities inhabited by younger, more educated people, tilt to the more global, democratic, progressive side of the political map. The rural areas lean towards to the conservative, radical, extreme right.

I will not assume that the people in the cities are smarter than the people in the rural areas, or that they have some extra knowledge that makes them more able to analyze the political situation. I would, however, claim that we shape our position depending on our analysis of our risks and opportunities, our identity, our class, our social status, and our self-esteem.

The fact that growing groups of individuals are now pushed more to the nationalist side is a result of narrowing opportunities, growing risk, lower social status, and lower self-esteem. If that is true, then moving people from one side of the political map to the other is a question of what kind of policies we adopt.

THE BIRTH OF A NATIONALIST[5]

For many years I have been an activist, a political player, and a member of the Israeli government. I always look for policies that can change things for the better. How can we influence patterns of voting? We know people shift allegiances: Trump was elected because people who voted for Obama moved to Trump. They are not going to stay Republicans forever; they can move back.

Globalism has failed many people. It could not replace the nation state as it could not answer the basic human needs the nation state fulfilled. The nation state is not ideal: maybe it is not here forever, maybe someday something totally different will emerge, maybe we will all be governed by artificial intelligence. But for the time being alternatives are rare, and nation states are essential even for the purpose of international collaboration, the revival of Europe, or for ecological matters. They are the building blocks we should work with. I am wholeheartedly against dismantling something we do not know how to replace.

I want to end with a word of optimism. A lot of people believe that the processes I have described have pushed voters to the right—to the extreme right—and nationalism is taking over. This is indeed true, for the moment. Yet despite the common assumption that the center is sinking and extremism has the upper hand, in reality the political picture is much more nuanced. I would like to suggest that we are going to see a rebalancing act. More and more political leaders are going to rethink their policies and make a move towards the center.

Some examples: Boris Johnson. I would not vote for Boris Johnson, but I listened carefully to his first speeches in the British House of Commons. The first thing he did is he looked at Jeremy Corbyn and said, "I'm going to steal some of your ideas. I'm going to work for the welfare state, I'm going to work for pensions, I'm going to lower taxes on houses, I'm going to take the social route, because I understand who my voters are." Then he said something else which is also quite uncommon for the conservative right: "I'm going to make England green." I do not know what he is going to do (it is early days), but he knows where the young audience is. This uncommon mélange of right and left, democratic and conservative, progressive and more traditional ideas creates a new kind of left-green nationalism that is becoming popular.

Let us now look at Denmark. What did Mette Frederiksen do to pull the rug out from under the Danish People's Party? She comes from the left, but she captured the attention of right-wing voters because she offered a clear vision of immigration. She took a national position on immigration while making a very clear commitment to welfarism and green policies.

Frederiksen may be leading the way in nurturing a conversation between traditional social democratic policies and what is more commonly seen as a right-wing nationalist position. Four defining features characterize this ideological mélange: a strong welfare state, a firm position on climate change, a hard line on immigration, and a commitment to put one's country first. While the first two are natural ingredients of a left-wing agenda, the latter two are much less obvious bedfellows.

Needless to say, support for the welfare state is a fundamental pillar of social democratic policies, and though it has come under attack in recent years, awareness of the social and political damage induced by growing social and economic gaps makes its necessity more obvious than ever. So much so, that even in less welfare-orientated states, policies favoring redistribution are gathering support, from proposals to impose a "rich tax" in the USA, to the inheritance tax in France, as well as the proliferation of new global taxation policies seeking to limit the ability of mega-companies to avoid paying taxes in those countries they operate in.

The second pillar, a firm position on climate change, is more of a newcomer. Younger people around the world are now more and more engaged in attempts to reduce the damage caused by previous generations, demanding that their governments adopt pro-environment policies, even if these imply some restrictions on consumption. Moving from a more short-term materialistic set of preferences to a more long-term one is certainly one of main features of the newly evolving social democratic way of thinking.

The connection between welfarism and ecological awareness is grounded in an understanding that just social policies must take into account the needs and rights of more than one generation. Both stress the fact that our political union is a transgenerational one. When we think about best political practices, we must try to solicit a commitment by present generations (today's taxpayers) to both former generations (today's pensioners) and future generations. In a way, the commitment to fight for a better eco-system could be seen as what the younger generations will receive in return for their willingness to support the elderly.

Welfarism and transgenerational concerns lead to the third pillar, commonly seen as grounded in national thinking—putting one's country first. An essential part of a working social contract is that all parties strive to cultivate the economy in order to create social capital that could benefit members, rewarding them for their collective efforts. Under such conditions, it will be natural for states to want to look inwardly, seeking to provide their members with tools for individual and collective development; hence, the logic of state investment in education, health, and support systems for those left behind.

Putting one's country first is therefore motivated by a sense of commitment for what we care about rather than from a sense of superiority. Of course, there are limits to what one can do in order to promote the well-being of one's fellow citizens, and one ought not to exploit or harm members of other political units in order to promote the wellbeing of one's own countrymen and women. Yet for the welfare state to survive and prosper it must retain a high level of social cohesion and a strong sense of continuity. Unless members see their future as tied up with that of the state, unless they believe they will raise children in this particular setting, unless they assume they will work and age in this social context, they will have no interest in investing in the collective wellbeing.

The process of forming an ongoing partnership is also the basis for the formation of a group/national identity that fosters feelings of togetherness, alongside pride in the nation's achievements and a commitment to make it great. One can now see how the fourth and final pillar of this new approach, a clear policy on membership and immigration, is a natural match to the first three. This also explains why "open door" or "welcoming" policies such as the ones espoused by Angela Merkel, which are threatening the continuity and stability of the welfare state, are likely to be rejected.

Hence it is not surprising that generous welfare states offer firm and well-defined immigration policies motivated by the needs of the state rather than by the needs of newcomers. Canada, a state that takes pride in its commitment to both welfare policies and immigration, selects its immigrants carefully and in a very instrumental way, while leaving room for a generous quota of refugees. The Nordic countries (except for Sweden) also offer a combination of generous welfarism and restrictive immigration policies. Attempts to combine open borders with a welfare state have backfired in two different ways: growing support for right-wing parties as well as attempts to restrict the universalism of the welfare state and make benefits conditional.

The political map is being shaken up. A new political convergence embedded in nationalism, putting one's country and the wellbeing of its citizens first, alongside green policies, seems to be emerging. In five years' time, we are likely to see a liberal, progressive nationalism, or left-wing nationalism, as the order of the day.

That is the optimistic version of what is happening now and I do see signs that it is about to happen. I think we, as people who can influence our societies, have a role to play in bringing it about. Acknowledging the way elites, maybe unintentionally, betrayed some of their duties to their people, we must ask ourselves how we are going to contribute to a process that allows more people to share in the opportunities we promised they will have. It is a challenge. If we meet this challenge, maybe we will be able to create a better political future for all of us.

Notes

1. I am talking only about the West, because things in the developing world are rather different.
2. The American Prospect using data provided by Branko Milanović. Miles Corak, "The Winners and Losers of Globalization: Branko Milanović's New Book on Inequality Answers Two Important Questions" in *American Prospect*, May 18, 2016.
3. McKinsey Global Institute Report, "Poorer Than Their Parents: Flat or Falling Incomes in Advanced Economies," 2016. www.mckinsey.com/global-themes/employment-and-growth/poorer-than-their-parents-a-new-perspective-on-income-inequality (accessed January 20, 2020); See also Ray Chetty, Maximilian Hell, Nathaniel Hendren, Robert Manduca, and Jimmy Narang, "The Fading American Dream: Trends in Absolute Income Mobility Since 1940" in *Opportunity Insights*, 2016.

https://opportunityinsights.org/paper/the-fading-american-dream (accessed January 16, 2020).

4. Harry G. Frankfurt, *On Inequality* (Princeton: Princeton University Press, 2015), p. 1.

5. See Yael Tamir, *Why Nationalism* (Princeton: Princeton University Press, 2019), p. 125.

CHAPTER 5

EUROPEAN VALUES AND GOOD LEADERSHIP: FACING UP TO ROLE DISTANCE

TIMO MEYNHARDT

Europe is first and foremost an intellectual concept. Since Greco-Roman antiquity, various myths, peace projects, and crises have been associated with it, and there have been geographical, political, and economic attempts to contain it. Increasingly, Europe is about collective experiences and the strengthening of cultural ties. In current models of thought generally, the European idea has become important as an identity-creating space of experiences and values.

Under the international law of the 2007 Lisbon Treaty, the Member States of the European Union emphasized and laid down six particular values for Europe: respect for human dignity, freedom, democracy, equality, the rule of law, and respect for human rights. This set of values can be seen as the expression of a common decision-making process and, through its inclusion in the Treaty, it has provided the European Union with guidance for action. Given that violations of these fundamental values can be punished by the suspension of EU membership, the scope of this commitment is clear.

Today, these shared values form fundamental axes in European countries' political and legal systems. In the global community, they are likely to prove an advantage in terms of cultural survival, if they can be successfully promoted and implemented in the population at large.

However, from a sociological and psychological point of view, we must always re-examine how these values are actually lived and what effect they have in the world of experience. Without an inner affirmation, even the best idea remains an intellectual construct unconnected to emotions and motivations. It is a simple thing, but hard to do. Acting upon it is a Sisyphean task, but it is essential.

Decision-makers in politics, businesses, and organizations in particular are required to use their behavior to create incentives, exploit potential, and moderate responsibly in situations where conflicts and areas of tension arise. The social elites especially must be able to explain why they are doing what they are doing.

The fundamental European values go hand-in-hand with tolerance, justice, solidarity, and other Humanist values. While this range of values may sound easy to endorse, its implementation is subject to many conditions and freighted with conflict. A mechanism is therefore required that goes beyond or complements principle-based evaluations. Thinking in terms of dilemmas and the associated idea of choosing the lesser evil quickly runs up against limits in a world of plural values in which contradictions and paradoxes must inevitably be tolerated.

In this essay, I would like to use concepts from role theory to show how executives can deal with irreconcilable contradictions and value conflicts. The answer lies in the maintenance of one's own identity through *sovereign role distance*. Humanist values are most likely enforceable when the actors involved consistently address their own values and acknowledge what is right or wrong from their point of view. A certain amount of distance is required in order to be able to look at oneself from within the role, and to look at the role from within oneself.

Put negatively, what appears to be a lack of identification with the task or the values, is in positive terms the key to good self-leadership and thus a prerequisite for good leadership in general. The Leipzig Leadership Model serves as the basis for these ideas.

EUROPEAN VALUES IN THE LEIPZIG LEADERSHIP MODEL

There is no European style of leadership as the intellectual traditions are too diverse. However, it could be worthwhile to make use of the inherently Humanist orientation of fundamental European values to create an image of "good leadership." One current example of this is the Leipzig Leadership Model (LLM)[1] which translates culturally deep-rooted, historical European values into issues of leadership. These values include the balance between freedom and responsibility, a personal commitment to liberal ideas that can be adhered to, and the quest for the common good in the area of tension between autonomy and dependence.

The premises of the LLM include a concept of the individual that is characterized by respect for the dignity of each person and their right to personal freedom and participation. This is underpinned by a normative starting point, which asserts that it is a great achievement of civilization that in a liberal system people can determine their own goals, and the latter are not prescribed from above. Without a broad consensus about the requirements of a functioning society, however, this is not viable and the individual cannot thrive.

This model can also be applied to companies and other organizations that need a license to operate in order to achieve long-term effectiveness. Entrepreneurial freedom and responsibility are mutually dependent and should go hand-in-hand from the start. The very European notion of placing business thinking and activities at the service of society resonates in these ideas, for example in the role model of the "honorable merchant," as seen in medieval Italy and the north German cities of the Hanseatic League in the territory of present-day Europe.

In the LLM, these intellectual traditions have been incorporated and contextualized in social scientific terms:

> The model also goes hand-in-hand with the conviction that, in a fundamentally unmanageable world, it is important to remain capable of acting and to develop

> an attitude that is defined by a value contribution and not by status, knowledge, or power. Conversely, the model offers a way of giving meaning to one's own status, knowledge, or power.[2]

A value contribution arises from concrete action: whoever contributes, leads. Those who do not contribute, do not lead; or, if you want to lead, you have to contribute. Seeing yourself as part of a greater whole and finding your own role within it focuses simultaneously on self-commitment and self-transcendence.

In the LLM, executives (of the future) are encouraged not only to base their social role on the expectations of colleagues and the organization, but also on the needs of society as a whole, and to see themselves as the recipient of social role expectations. In this context, Peter Drucker, the father of modern management studies, spoke about the "social function" that is inherent in every leadership function.[3] It is particularly important for executives to accept the social expectations associated with their role and to embody this role.

In this model, integrated thinking in general stands for the European tradition of thought. Put simply, an executive should always ask themselves four questions and be able to find coherent solutions:

1. Purpose (why?): Are we pursuing an overarching goal?

2. Entrepreneurial spirit (how?): Are we thinking and acting in an entrepreneurial way?

3. Responsibility (how?): Are our activities legitimate?

4. Effectiveness (what?): Are we effective?

The purpose of good leadership focuses on social issues. This contribution logic transforms the question of "why?", the core question of purpose, into the question of "what for?". Internal affirmation and (self-)determination lead to the question of what it means for a greater whole. A purpose does not exist for its own sake. It cannot focus solely on the individualistic self, but seeks fulfillment by contributing to the broadest possible primary principle, the common good. The answer to "why" therefore remains incomplete unless it includes the view from outside.

The conflicts inherent in such a holistic approach are obvious. While leadership that focuses on effectiveness is more geared towards optimizing existing processes, leadership in the spirit of entrepreneurship emphasizes creative freedom and the necessary willingness to take risks to develop new processes. And not every purpose can be implemented in a responsible manner. A purpose that can only be achieved through irresponsible action is prohibited. The "how" of the responsibility dimension is therefore not strictly subordinate to the "why" and/or "what for," but it restricts it as well. This guideline informs the principle of *primum non nocere*, borrowed from the Hippocratic Oath and applied to leadership challenges.

In practice, it is not always possible to find a balance between the areas of tension brought into focus by this approach to leadership and find beneficial solutions. A compromise based on mutual respect does not mean capitulating to reality, but rather is a considerable achievement within the framework of the fundamental European values we mentioned above, an achievement in which values cannot simply be played off against each other—not freedom *or* equality, but freedom *and* equality.

In the event of a conflict or even a crisis, the immediate challenge for an executive is to get a grip and find their bearings, because only if one's own activity chimes with one's self-image can one's own actions make sense, and only then can one serve as a role model for others. By engaging with the LLM in their curriculum, students rehearse how European values can be lived out in day-to-day leadership. Finding the ideal solution is not the most important thing, but rather a feeling for the right questions that focus one's own attention on what is feasible.

THE SOCIAL ROLE BETWEEN ELEMENTARY CATEGORY AND BEHAVIORAL SHELL

In today's postmodern world, we emphasize the scope available for creating social roles. Everything seems possible; everything is a question of attribution and individual initiative. But in so doing we occasionally overlook the fact that, in addition to any subjective determination and individual interpretation of roles, objective circumstances also limit the scope for action. This applies to the practical constraints that exist in an organizational context as a result of the legal framework or the functional context. The form in which individuality is possible is objectively specified in this sense and is not simply an attribution that might easily be changed. An executive cannot escape these expectations or just cherry-pick certain aspects of the role. Neither is the executive free from the personal biographical and cultural characteristics that they bring to their performance of the role.

In the most general way, the concept of "social role" stands for the sum of the expectations that a person in a specific social position must deal with in a social context. Role requirements describe what a person typically thinks, feels, and does and/or should do in a role. The person is confronted with requirements and, in the best-case scenario, can also "grow" as a person with the role. Roles connect the individual to their social environment, helping them to contribute to the creation of the environment. Just as the individual experiences role expectations as facilitating their orientation, so by performing their role they maintain the associated expectations and contribute to the production and reproduction of social structures.

It is not surprising that the concept of role in sociology appeared early on in the work of one of the discipline's founding fathers, Ferdinand Tönnies. For Tönnies, the role is an intellectual artifact, through which a new element of formalization and distance in a person's relationship with him or herself comes into play. He writes:

> Every individual is the natural representative of his own person. The concept of the person cannot be derived from any other empirical egos than the individual people. For in so far as every individual is endowed with thought and will, he is perceivable.

Consequently, there are real and natural persons in so far as there exist human beings who conceive themselves as such, accept and play this "role," each one assuming the "character" of a person like a mask held before his face.[4]

For Tönnies, the form of a role already exists within the *idea of the person*:

> ... a unity by external determination, *unum per accidens*, mechanical unity. That is to say, in the same way as a formation of rational will has reality and unity only for the person possessing it, and through its relation to possible results, the concept of the person is a figment, a product of scientific thought. It is intended to express the unity of the origin of such formations, i.e. the disposition of a complex of force, power, means.[5]

Just as the individual has to build a definable form of a role as part of their consistent experience as a *person* in order to be able to slip into a variety of social roles, a community is organized on the basis of many different roles. Role expectations create a certain degree of reliability and enable social ties. The sociologist Ralf Dahrendorf even gave this a name—*homo sociologicus*:

> Every position carries with it certain expected modes of behavior; every position a person occupies requires him to do certain things and exhibit certain

characteristics; to every social position there belongs a *social role*. By assuming a social position, the individual becomes a character in the drama written by the society he is living in. With every position he assumes, society hands him a role to play.[6]

It is no coincidence that Dahrendorf precedes his description with a quotation from Shakespeare:

All the world's a stage,
And all the men and women merely players:
They have their exits, and their entrances;
And one man in his time plays many parts...

(*As You Like It*, Act 2, Scene 7)

Without a doubt, the concept of the role, as borrowed from the theater, offers a perspective for understanding leadership challenges. It would be an exaggeration to see the role concept alone as the one fundamental category for understanding leadership behavior or, conversely, to ignore the idea of the social role as an empty behavioral shell. Containing elements of "must," "shall," and "can," role expectations are not unambiguous, nor can anyone seriously deny the reality of role effects and conflicts. Indeed, the terminology is enshrined in everyday language. We speak of "slipping into a role," "disappearing into a role," "casting off a role," or "behaving out of character."

In any case, the separation between role and person seems appropriate for understanding situations in which different expectations collide and orientation factors do not depend solely on the participants. While a typical recommendation would be to negotiate expectations, here I would like to look at a kind of reserve capacity that exists within the person—sovereign role distance.

ROLE DISTANCE AS A BALANCING ACT

The contradictions that exist within all the expectations placed on executives often cannot be resolved. By this we mean both the conflict between the individual's demands on themselves and external expectations (intra-role conflict), as well as the conflict between different expectations that are placed on a person with different roles (inter-role conflict). It is easy enough to say that the source of innovation and progress lies in the power of the conflict itself. But this requires an ability to reflect clearly about oneself, because if you cannot cope with yourself, you won't be able to cope with others.

If the contradictions in expectations are not even noticed, there is a risk of direct identification, without maintaining any internal distance, which can lead to the individual feeling overwhelmed and being accused of submissiveness. The first step is to be aware of roles, i.e. to perceive a pattern of expectations that has been set up externally and that requires an adjustment in one's own behavior.

A role wants to be accepted, learned, developed, and thus performed. If, in so doing, the executive experiences themselves not only as performing a role, but can also reflect as a spectator on their own behavior, then they immediately become aware that interaction with others is being mediated into becoming a certain role as a result of their own relationship, and how his happens. The social role then quickly becomes an empty behavioral shell or a character mask, which risks a weakened sense of identification with the role.

The perceived role distance between self and role can be interpreted as alienation from the role and a desire for independence from it.[7] Perhaps the role was never seriously accepted internally or there is a basic lack of understanding of it. In a positive sense, deliberate role distance can be a sign of sovereign identification, which in itself makes it possible to react playfully and creatively to new situations. Such "role play" does not negate the contradictions in expectations, but highlights the possibilities and limits of the role itself.

As paradoxical as it sounds, authenticity only arises when the conflicting nature of expectations is addressed. One example of this is to convincingly articulate the difference between a pragmatic solution and the noble ideals of contributing to the greater whole. The executive can be seen as a person playing a role without negating the parameters of the role. Indeed, a coherent leadership performance consists in not eliminating the distance between "role" and "true self" in one direction or the other, but in maintaining the tension and developing oneself alongside the contradictions.

Whether caused by pressure to conform or lack of a strong ego, without an inner sense of distance with regard to role expectations the individual would be completely absorbed in their role and would no longer be recognizable as an individual person. In such a case the individual *is* the role, and the famous "character mask" has taken root. Being consolidated in a role does not have to be a disadvantage initially, provided that fulfilling the role stabilizes self-image and is functionally important for a person (e.g. someone in a new job). In addition, only by internalizing the role can the role be managed flexibly. Or to put it another way: improvisation is the result of many hours of practice, and an effortless ability to develop the role is the result of previous efforts. But danger also lurks here: if the role is performed without a minimum of internal sympathy and involvement, there is a risk of manipulation and deception. Professionally necessary role distance (for example in the work of doctors, therapists, or teachers) can turn into superficial role play. Too much distance leads to experiences of alienation and inner withdrawal. Above all, however, a lack of role identification is unsettling to one's interlocutors, because they cannot rely on the certainty of expectations that the role implies.

What is required, therefore, is a constant balancing act between personal and social identity, between inner guidance and obstinacy on the one hand, and on the other the willingness to face up to the requirements of the role without any ifs or buts. In their efforts to assert their identity, the executive gives the impression "of a constantly juggling and balancing artist, an actor who can control everything on stage at one moment and then quietly steal away, a skilled dealer who secures his contracts with all kinds of get-out clauses and then puts all his eggs in one basket, almost a charlatan, who in his ambiguous comments won't ultimately commit to anything."[8]

This balance between the portrayal of "self" and "other," or between "mask" and "true self," expresses the contradictory nature of expectations, norms, and perspectives that stimulates and provokes change. Consistency is created by revealing potentials and tensions. In other words, the individual overcomes psychological unease (experience of dissonance) by not fully taking on board the role requirements and/or creating distance from them. This mental mechanism of objectification increases the possibility of regaining consonance in one's own thoughts and feelings. If this is not successful, the ability to act is lost.

However, dealing flexibly with different expectations is only productive if it creates a credible balance that can meet expectations and yet contribute something special. This means not going over the top, but rather finding the point where an executive is both like everyone else and yet completely unique—in other words successful identity work.

The famous actor Bernhard Minetti was once asked how he managed…

> …to remain in the limelight in major roles across political eras and changing styles. His secret has been his versatility as an actor. Over the decades, his versatility has been nourished by his extraordinary ability to absorb inspiration from his environment, for

example by making bygone styles and fashions his own and thus shaping his personality and acting. For example, on stage he is always of the moment and at the same time an actor through whose idiosyncratic presence German theater has remained alive for almost a century... To rediscover a role, to imagine it differently from before, nourished by his curiosity for people, that is one of the driving forces of this actor, who works rationally, not from gut feeling. He sees himself as an executor of the author. Not by unreservedly identifying with his character, but by performing the character with extreme sensitivity. He is interested, he says, in "their vulnerability more than their bourgeois morality, their bourgeois truthfulness. Both chime with my fundamental feeling that we are not entirely certain of ourselves, just as the world is not certain. That sounds like evasion, like not wanting to come to grips with things. That would be the wrong conclusion. I have a great sense of responsibility, it is part of my discipline as well as my existence; [...] But I also have within me another feeling—that ultimately I cannot be grasped."[9]

SUMMARY: ROLE DISTANCE AS A PERFORMANCE FACTOR IN GOOD LEADERSHIP

The perception and acceptance of a basic tension between role and person is a key skill in meeting the enormous requirements of a contradictory practice.

If you do not take account of this and make use of it, you are not fully exploiting the possibilities of your own effectiveness. Undoubtedly, the ideas of social role theory prove to be a useful tool for understanding successful (self)-leadership. We can now sum up our argument: commitment to a role makes flexibility in a role possible! Only mastering a role requirement enables a real, creative development of the relationship between freedom (developing personal identity) and responsibility (implementation of the role requirement).

In short, for the kind of leadership based on European values as translated into the Leipzig Leadership Model, a constant balancing act between person and role is a necessary condition for finding innovative solutions and thus cultural viability.

The ego identity gained through awareness of one's own and others' expectations of one's own role enables an executive to determine the balance between dependency and autonomy. This is what is meant by sovereign role distance: engaging with the requirements of the social role and at the same time experiencing oneself as a person with self-will. The existential experience of one's own characteristics ("true self," "self") promotes real empathy with and humility towards others, as well as an understanding of one's dependence on others.

Self-respect is the prerequisite and the consequence of respect for the dignity of others.

Establishing and maintaining a difference between a social role and oneself is an essential part of competent self-management. It is not about playing one against each other, but about gaining orientation by clarifying roles and the resulting degrees of freedom of thought, feeling, and acting.

If, for example, both alternatives in a decision appear to be wrong, sovereign role distance allows a creative view of how the tension inherent in the situation can be used productively and new things can be created by an intellectual combination of opposites. Overcoming "either-or" logic and/or a dilemma also requires the strength to develop and advocate one's own values. Echoing the Kantian Enlightenment motto of *sapere aude*, the executive is encouraged and obliged to "think for themselves."

Notes

1. Manfred Kirchgeorg, Timo Meynhardt, Andreas Pinkwart, Andreas Suchanek, and Henning Zülch, *Das Leipziger Führungsmodell*, 3rd revised edn. (Leipzig: HHL Leipzig Graduate School of Management, 2018).

2. Kirchgeorg et al., *Das Leipziger Führungsmodell*, p. V.

3. Peter F. Drucker, *Management: Tasks, Responsibilities, Practices* (New York: Harper Business, 1973).

4. Ferdinand Tönnies, *Community and Society*, trans. and ed. Charles P. Loomis (New York: Dover Publications, 2002), p. 175.

5. Tönnies, *Community and Society*, p. 173.

6. Ralf Dahrendorf, *Homo Sociologicus* (London: Routledge and Kegan Paul, 1973), p. 17.

7. Erving Goffman, *The Presentation of Self in Everyday Life* (New York: Doubleday & Company, 1959).

8. Lothar Krappmann, *Soziologische Dimensionen der Identität* (Stuttgart: Klett-Cotta Verlag, 1993), p. 56.

9. Gerhard Ebert, "Das Fragwürdige in unserem Tun" in *Neues Deutschland*, January 26, 1995, p. 12.

CHAPTER 6

MAKING BETTER USE OF EUROPE'S GREAT POTENTIAL

STEFAN OSCHMANN

"If Europe were once united in the sharing of its common inheritance, there would be no limit to the happiness, to the prosperity and the glory which its three or four hundred million people would enjoy."[1] Seventy-three years have passed since Winston Churchill made this point in his famous speech at the University of Zurich. But the message remains as valid today as it was in 1946.

A united Europe can achieve a great deal. This is especially true at a time when advances in digital technologies and biotechnology are fundamentally changing many aspects of our economic and social lives, and the geopolitical balance of power in our world is undergoing a lasting shift.

The European project, the European Union, is more important now than ever before. It ensures peace and freedom in Europe, and thus prosperity and economic growth. A European Union that enables economic progress within changing fiscal and political parameters can play a leading role in the world of the 21st century, above all when it comes to promoting scientific research and developing the technologies that we will need to achieve the United Nations Sustainable Development Goals.

EUROPE UNDER PRESSURE

For most of us in Europe, it was self-evident for many long years that European unification is irreversible. In recent years, however, we have been forced to realize that this was a false conclusion. The 2008 financial crisis, and the debt crises that it triggered, led to harsh economic and social sacrifices, above all in the countries of southern Europe. State budgets were drastically reduced, social benefits cut back, jobs eliminated. This led to major social upheaval, governments were punished, and political party systems changed considerably. We are still seeing the impacts of the crisis to this day, for example in the relatively high levels of unemployment among young people.

Many citizens of the EU feel that Europe can no longer provide answers to these urgent problems. As a consequence, populist and Eurosceptic political movements are gaining ground all over the continent. We saw what this can lead to around three and a half years ago in the United Kingdom, as a narrow majority cast their votes in favor of leaving the European Union.

In recent years, the economic situation in Europe has in fact improved somewhat. In 2018, the economy of the European Union grew by 2.2 percent. However, for the coming years, the current outlook is noticeably weaker. Moreover, productivity in Europe is growing too slowly in comparison with other countries such as the United States, and that in turn dampens long-term growth prospects.

A further challenge in Europe is demographic change. Rising life expectancies and declining birth rates are leading to significant aging of the population. Estimates indicate that by 2050 there will be only two working Europeans for every retired European. In addition to this structural demographic change, there is the influence of new technologies. Scenarios that predict a dramatic loss of jobs through technologies such as artificial intelligence seem exaggerated to me; nevertheless, it is clear that technological advances will lead to structural changes in the European labor market.

Europe is experiencing external economic pressures as well. On the one hand, there is a fundamental shift of the center of global economic gravity towards Asia. This will cause Europe to lose a certain amount of economic significance, relatively speaking. Another development, however, poses a much greater threat: the increasing rise of trade conflicts. Trade policy and market access issues are being instrumentalized in international political disputes to a much greater extent than was the case only a few years ago. For Merck, as for many other European companies with global value chains, this development is very problematic. And it is also a threat to Europe as a whole. We cannot and must not accept a situation in which the survival of the fittest prevails in international trade.

In light of all this, we must do more to promote Europe's economic growth. Europe's economy must become more productive. We need growth-friendly parameters on a long-term basis. And above all, this means that we need a European Union that is a leader in science and technology, and whose researchers and entrepreneurs rank among the global technological leaders. Such a Europe will flourish, ensure the prosperity of its citizens, and play a role in shaping the world of the 21st century.

A GOOD STARTING POSITION

The preconditions are not bad. Europe has top international universities, excellent research institutions, and many highly innovative companies. European researchers publish significantly more scientific papers than their colleagues in the United States and China. European companies account for about a quarter of all industrial investments in research and development, a share that has remained constant over the past ten years.

Europe has a very vibrant start-up scene. This is evident in the many excellent applications we receive for our Merck Accelerator program, which supports young start-up companies. And the data backs this up as well. According to the McKinsey Global Institute, the number of European start-ups in the field of Artificial Intelligence, for example, has tripled over the past three years. Investments in technology start-ups have also risen significantly, reaching a volume of US$23 billion in 2018.[2]

This is a good foundation, and now we need to build on it because the competition is not to be caught napping. Here too, the data is clear: according to the Organization for Economic Co-operation and Development (OECD), the 28 member states of the European Union spent of nearly 2 percent of their GDP on research and development in 2017. By comparison, the People's Republic of China spent well over 2 percent, while the figure for the United States was almost 3 percent.[3] Companies in the United States, China, and Korea are investing significantly more in research and development today than they did some years ago. And in terms of important future-oriented technologies such as quantum computers and synthetic biology, studies show that Europe is falling behind countries such as the United States and China.[4]

Europe has many successful companies operating in the digital sector. But here as well, a comparison shows that Europe is not among the global leaders. According to a study by the management consulting firm McKinsey, for example, US companies earn a much higher share of their revenues with digital products.[5] Even with regard to the so-called unicorns—unlisted start-ups valued by investors at over US$1 billion—Europe lags behind. There are 156 such companies in the United States, 91 in China, and only 36 in Europe.

After years of American dominance, China is now emerging as a strong new competitor. Not only do the numbers show this; if you walk the streets of major Chinese cities such as Beijing, Shanghai, or Shenzhen today, you can feel it.

What can we in Europe do? First of all, Europe, despite its deficits, has a great deal to be proud of. The Industrial Revolution began here. Europe is the home of the kind of Enlightenment thinking that enabled the economic and technological progress of the past centuries. And today's European Union has unique strengths as well: great cultural diversity, a strong tradition of democracy and the rule of law, as well as a culture of collaboration and cooperation. Nowhere else can these traits be found in the same combination. We should build on these strengths in order to jointly rise to the future challenges that Europe faces. From a business perspective, the steps to be taken seem clear.

DRIVE INNOVATION

Take a look at the creation and history of today's leading innovation hubs and it quickly becomes clear that these high-tech centers are not emerging as a result of the invisible hand of the market alone. Whether in

Silicon Valley in the United States, in China's Pearl River Delta, or in Israel, a substantial amount of state support invariably played and continues to play a very important role. The European Union should therefore promote scientific and technological innovation to a much greater extent than it has up to now.

Naturally, this primarily concerns European budgetary planning. Research, development, and innovation should be priorities in the European Union's budget for the period between 2021 and 2027. With the Horizon Europe program, the European Commission has presented a sound proposal for the promotion of research and development in the coming years. However, the amount of €100 billion proposed to date should be increased further. The European Round Table of Industrialists recommends a budget of €120 billion.

While money is important, it is by no means everything. Sound cross-sectoral collaboration among researchers plays at least as great a role. A perfect example here is the Innovative Medicines Initiative (IMI). The largest public-private partnership in the life sciences field, IMI is sponsored and financed by the European Union and by EFPIA, the European Federation of Pharmaceutical Industries and Associations. The public sector and private companies each contribute roughly half of the initiative's budget. In the period between 2014 and 2020, the partners are investing a total of €3.3 billion. The participating institutions come from a diverse range of sectors and include universities, non-university research institutions, as well as large and medium-sized companies. In the framework of the initiative, they collaborate, for example, at the so-called pre-competitive stage, e.g. on new processes for the development of medicines. In addition, IMI takes on the development of new therapies in areas in which individual companies have only limited economic incentives, the best example here being new antibiotics.

The most important point is that the collaboration in the framework of IMI is highly successful and has been met with acceptance both in science and in industry. The various projects underway as part of the initiative are working on very promising topics, including the identification of genes that play an important role in the development of Alzheimer's, new approaches to the treatment of rheumatoid arthritis, and new ways to combat drug-resistant bacteria in hospitals. Cross-sectoral collaboration has paid off in the pharmaceutical industry. We should further strengthen such cooperation in Europe in the coming years, in many more specialized areas.

In addition, we need a regulatory framework in Europe that enhances and consistently promotes the pace of scientific and technological development. The "fit for innovation" principle can play an important role here, as it can be used to assess whether regulations promote innovation, or at least do not create any new barriers to it.

BRING THE EUROPEAN SINGLE MARKET TO COMPLETION

The European Single Market, the guaranteed free movement of goods, services, people, and capital, is one of the greatest achievements of the European Union. The economic shared value is clear, and hardly any other country benefits from the European Single Market to as great an extent as Germany. Studies show that income gains through the Single Market amount to well over €80 billion—every year.[6]

The advantages of the Single Market, however, go far beyond the economic aspects. In my view, the freedom to live and work in any Member State in particular makes an essential contribution towards strengthening a shared European identity.

The European Single Market is not yet complete. In the case of digital technology companies especially, however, it is important that they be able to rapidly expand, or scale, their business operations. Here, the United States and China still have an advantage over Europe due to their sheer size. The European Union should therefore do all it possibly can to eliminate differences in national regulations and to complete the Single Market, especially in the digital area. A market with around 450 million relatively prosperous consumers is a major strategic resource for Europe that should be utilized much better than it is today.

The EU General Data Protection Regulation (GDPR) shows that a Europe-wide, uniform regulation can be a competitive advantage. With this regulation, the European Union has set a global standard in data protection towards which other countries such as Australia and Brazil are now orienting their policies. The high level of data protection can be an important argument in favor of Europe, particularly with regard to new business models that involve sensitive data, such as in the health sector. Europe should now go a step further and give scientists and companies access to anonymized public-sector data pools, for example in the health or transport sectors. This would be an interesting way of promoting research and supporting new business models.

MAKE TRADE POLICIES OPEN AND FAIR

The European Union needs free and fair global trade. Foreign trade accounts for more than 30 percent of Europe's GDP. Today, many European companies have international value-added chains.

Against this background, the European Union should strive to promote an open and rules-based world trade order and should throw its full economic weight behind this aim. Not the survival of the fittest, but rather the rule of law must once again prevail. Because one thing is clear: trade wars may lead to one-sided gains in the short term, but in the long run, nobody wins—and ultimately everyone loses. The goal of European trade policy must therefore be to eliminate customs and trade barriers and to ensure fair competitive conditions for both European and non-European companies. This applies particularly with regard to large and important trading partners such as the United States and China. On a global level, the European Union should take the lead in terms of reforming, and thus strengthening, the World Trade

Organization (WTO). This includes an effective system for the arbitration of trade disputes.

Another key issue for Europe is the future relationship with Great Britain after Brexit. The relationship should be as close and as seamless as possible.

SEE MAJOR TOPICS AS OPPORTUNITIES

From an economic perspective, there are many reasons for supporting a strong, united, effective Europe. But if the Eurosceptic debates of recent years have shown us anything at all, it is that economic and rational arguments alone are not enough to generate sufficient support, let alone enthusiasm, for the European project among the public. Pointing to 70 years of peaceful development, as valuable as it is, is also losing its pull in a population that takes peace for granted, and which largely knows war only through the media. We thus need something more in order to spark renewed enthusiasm for the European project—we need a positive future- and opportunity-oriented story of Europe.

To this end, Europe, and Europeans, should unite to take on the challenges of our time, because major, ambitious goals can give meaning, spark enthusiasm, and set energy free. Climate change, and mastering its impact, can be a major goal of this kind. The president of the European Commission, Ursula von der Leyen, has recognized this. Talking about this topic in her first speech before the European Parliament, she was clear in emphasizing that: "We must go further. We must strive for more."[7] That is only possible if we work together. Individual European countries, even the large ones such as Germany and France, can achieve little with regard to climate change by going at it alone. A united Europe, however, can play an important pioneering role at a global level, namely with regard to all United Nations Sustainable Development Goals.

To achieve these goals, we need new technologies in areas such as electronics, IT, biotech, architecture, mobility, and agriculture, and many more. Only through new, much more efficient technologies that minimize the use of resources can we keep our consumption of natural resources in check, and at the same time allow an increasing number of people to live in prosperity.

As far as the legislative framework is concerned, Europe is already a pioneer. It is the only major economic region in the world that has established the legal preconditions for the achievement of the goals of the Paris Agreement. Now European scientists and companies must set standards in new, efficient technologies that conserve resources. In this way, we can create economic growth, open up opportunities for many people in Europe, and at the same time spark new enthusiasm for the European project.

SET THE RIGHT PRIORITIES NOW

Today, Europe is facing major challenges. Populist and Eurosceptic movements, an increasingly aging society, the impact of the digital revolution, a new geopolitical balance of power—Europe, above all those who bear positions of responsibility in European politics, economics, and society, must find answers to all of these issues. My own answer is clear: Europe should make much better use of its great potential. Our many creative researchers and entrepreneurs, our excellent universities and research institutions, our vibrant start-up scene, our many leading technology companies—if we succeed in creating the best possible framework conditions for them and connecting their work with an opportunity- and future-oriented narrative, we will spark new enthusiasm for the European idea. And then we will be taking an important step towards enabling Europe to compete successfully in the new imperial world order in the years and decades to come.

Notes

1. Winston Churchill, "Zurich University Speech," September 19, 1946. https://www.churchill-in-zurich.ch/site/assets/files/1807/rede_winston_churchill_englisch.pdf (accessed December 4, 2019).

2. McKinsey Global Institute, "Innovation in Europe: Changing the Game to Regain a Competitive Edge," October 2019, p. 6. https://www.mckinsey.com/~/media/McKinsey/Featured%20Insights/Innovation/Reviving%20innovation%20in%20Europe/MGI-Innovation-in-Europe-Discussion-paper-Oct2019-vF.ashx (accessed November 28, 2019).

3. OECD, "Main Science and Technology Indicators." https://www.oecd-ilibrary.org/science-and-technology/data/oecd-science-technology-and-r-d-statistics/main-science-and-technology-indicators_data-00182-en (accessed November 28, 2019).

4. McKinsey Global Institute, "Innovation in Europe," p. 4.

5. McKinsey Global Institute, "Innovation in Europe," p. 9.

6. Süddeutsche Zeitung, "Deutschland profitiert vom Binnenmarkt wie kein anderes EU Land," May 8, 2019. https://www.sueddeutsche.de/wirtschaft/eu-binnenmarkt-profiteure-1.4437278 (accessed November 28, 2019).

7. Ursula von der Leyen, https://ec.europa.eu/commission/presscorner/detail/en/SPEECH_19_4230 (accessed November 27, 2019).

CHAPTER 7

EUROPE'S STRATEGIC AUTONOMY IN DIGITAL TECHNOLOGIES: PIPE DREAM OR REALISTIC VISION?

ROBERTO VIOLA

Digital technologies will change everything. We need to think about these changes and why Europe has to be a leader. And we must ask what kind of strategy Europe needs to pursue to make this happen.

To measure the challenge ahead, we can think about the future of the car industry. Consider a car in 1980. We could easily have said "Europe owns the key to all the technologies in this car," and we were able to provide the best cars in the world in the 1980s. Then think of a car today. I would say that we produce roughly 70 percent of the technology for the best cars in the world. Then think of a car in ten years from now. It's going to be a supercomputer on four wheels. Do we master fast electronics and data processing in Europe? Do we excel in advanced AI algorithms? Do we have all the knowledge about electric propulsion? Do we have enough production capacity for the batteries of the future? Consider the car in the year 2035: will it be a car we own in terms of the value chain, or will it depend on choices being made somewhere else? I'm talking here about one of the proudest flagships of our European industrial engineering and production.

The European Central Bank's July 2019 statement made clear that there is little reason to celebrate Europe's economy.[1] But it's not just the European economy that is struggling; the whole world's economy is. We are entering an economic cycle that is more complicated than the last five years. Unfortunately, Europe is slowing down and some countries are slowing down more than others, and these are the big countries. Most of the world's new economic growth will be linked to the digital transformation. If the slowdown of the economy is a problem, then the low level of digitalization is an even bigger problem for Europe. To sustain what is our crown jewel, the welfare state, we need to generate a lot of added value, and that means technology and products.

If we are not able to internalize the value, generate that value for ourselves, we will effectively not be able to sustain our social structure. One might say digitalization is for geeks, or that we will never learn how the smartphone works. But it is much more than that. It's about the way we produce things, the way we produce value, and the way our life is organized.

The digital economy generates value through externalities created by large platforms, and some of those platforms are owned by companies that are the largest in the world by market capitalization. One may wonder sometimes, are they corporations or are they states within states? Platforms know everything about our life. The dark side and the bright side, the public sphere and the private sphere. They know even more than the state does.

And with politics now being influenced by social media, these platforms have a crucial role in the political decision-making process, in terms of influencing democratic elections. Furthermore, some large platforms are active in shaping the future of crypto assets: take Facebook for example and its Libra project. In other words, there is an interest in "printing digital money." Looking at all these activities, one might be tempted to conclude that these mega-platforms have more power than the state. And none of these mega-platforms is European.

On the other side of the spectrum there are worrying trends in which states are using these new digital technologies to control people, to actually limit the freedom of expression, and to make sure that technological supremacy can be achieved. For example, over the last few years important value chains have been systematically replaced by Chinese technology.

At the moment, Europe is stuck in the middle. On one hand, we have the large corporations that are crunching our data and our lives; this is one model. On the other, there's the Chinese model, which is basically digital dominance. Should Europe be worried? I would say, yes, it is very worrying. The multilateral approach is not dead, but we are in a situation where the question is who wants technology as a card to play on the table.

The EU and its Member States combined are the largest aid donor in the world. We still have a rather romantic view about development: we think that development comes in stages and that we can help to build roads, then electric grids, and only at a later stage does technology become relevant. Of course, this is not the way it works. Cellphones have changed Africa.

They are changing the shape of the African economy at the speed of light—and not just Africa. Who is providing this technology? Not Europe.

Europe is building nice roads and helping with very important social developments, but we are rather absent in terms of technology, cellphones, mobile applications, and all these things that are changing the face of the developing world. Is it in our interests to be more active? Most certainly, yes. If we help to keep knowledge in Africa, if we help to build the digital infrastructure there, people will be able to work, the economy will grow faster, and people will have more reasons to stay rather than risk their life crossing the sea.

So we all have a collective interest, not only because we are the largest donor in the world, but also because the development of Africa is closely linked to the stability of Europe and its ability to sustain migration flows in a much better way. These two issues are deeply interlinked. Our experience of introducing digital identity to Kenya has been impressively positive. Through digital ID, Kenya is starting to understand its population, how many people there are, how they move, and has also started to introduce e-invoicing in order to have a much more transparent administration.

In Central Africa there is a European supercomputer. It predicts how the Niger River flows, which is very important to the nomadic population because they can move to higher ground before the river floods. In this way, we are saving lives and increasing people's quality of life. And through precision agriculture, a combination of satellite images, drones, Internet, and sensors, we can really change agriculture in Africa and make it more sustainable and self-sufficient.

Is there a European approach to digital development that will help us to help other countries more effectively and at the same time defend our own interests in the world? First, let me stress that Europe's starting position is not bad. Our internal market, which is increasingly transforming into a digital Single Market, is the wealthiest in the world: five hundred and thirty million people—not the largest in terms of population, but the largest by far in terms of wealth. The Single Market is a big asset.

Second, we are still number one in the world in car electronics, partly because we have supported the microelectronic industry with public funds. Sometimes state aid is necessary, especially when the rest of the world does the same. And in microelectronics, the rest of the world indeed does the same. They use defense contracts, they use supercomputing programs to develop the next-generation chips, and they pour billions of Euros into microelectronics. I believe the European Commission needs to play the same game—and in fact when we started to do that it made a difference. Our next step will be to develop a European capacity for fast processors.

When it comes to delivering public services, Europe is probably the most advanced region in terms of digital banking systems, transport systems, and healthcare. I think if we successfully digitalize these public services, we can send a clear message to the world—as well as making our citizens happy. In fact, digitalizing healthcare is a triple win. First, because of personalized medicine. Doctors will be able to experiment if a cure works or not on your "digital self," rather than on your "physical self." The way medicine works today is you go to the doctor and the doctor says "this pill might work; if it doesn't, call me." In ten years' time, you will go to the doctor with your smartphone and inside your smartphone there will be a genome sequencer that will allow the doctor to test, via a supercomputer, how well a particular remedy will work on your digital twin. The first win from digitalizing the healthcare sector is personalized medicine. This means finding answers to some illnesses we cannot yet cure and a better quality of life.

The second win is for the state. Today, we are spending, more or less, slightly below 10 percent of

GDP on healthcare in Europe. In Germany, Italy and France we are already at around 10 percent; in other countries it's around 6–7 percent. But it's continuing to rise because we live longer.[1] What is the answer to increasing healthcare costs? The only solution is technology: digitalizing healthcare. There is evidence that digitalizing healthcare brings a costs reduction of 20 percent—that's 2 percent of GDP, a huge amount.

The third win is for the healthcare sector as a whole. Healthcare is one of the most important industries for Europe. Keeping this sector strong is therefore another win.

I could go on. I could go on about digitalization in the automotive sector, in the banking sector, or in the transport sector. If Europe changes gear and starts looking at public services, looking at the economy at large, and how to transform them digitally, we can create our own digital path, differentiating us from the "digital imperialism" approach of some, or the large influence of a few powerful players from the private sector.

This is not just a dream, this is a reality. We are considered to be the best in the world when it comes to digital rulemaking. We have got to grips with data protection, we have fought hard to improve copyright regulation, and we have probably the best cyber-security regulations in the world. What we need to do now is improve the way we work together. Such a new method of working together has been tested in the field of supercomputers.

Supercomputers can change your life: for instance, synthesizing a new drug on a supercomputer takes just 30 minutes. With normal computers, this would take closer to 300 years. This is the type of thing that a supercomputer can do. A supercomputer can spot a cyber-attack in three to ten minutes. Normally it takes much longer, sometimes as much as three to four days. Supercomputers are therefore very important. In the past, we had a German supercomputer program, a French supercomputer program, an Italian one, a Spanish one, and so on. As a result, if you look at the list of the top 20 supercomputers in the world, the first EU country to make the list is Germany at number nine.[2]

Therefore, we, the European Commission, convinced Member States to do something very strange—work together. Let's federate our efforts, we said. And in just one year, we created the legal entity necessary for this new way of working and freed up €500 million in EU funding for it. The remaining capital needed came from the Member States, and now, after just twelve months, we have €1 billion available. In July 2019, we announced eight new supercomputing sites in Europe with the aim of making Europe number one.

So we can do it. But of course this did not happen by accident. It took willingness—political willingness—to come together to create something better than we could do separately. People forget that second part of the story. If you just put failing companies together and hope in that way to create a new European Facebook or Google, it would be a disaster. It takes political willingness, working together, and a product with real potential. We will repeat this success with computers, we will repeat it with microprocessors, and we will repeat it with advances in healthcare, if we federate our efforts. But if we play solo, I'm afraid we will not go very far and that applies to people as well. If you look at the ranking of technical schools in Europe post-Brexit, you will discover that we will not appear in the top 20.

This is a collective tragedy. In Europe, we should have the best engineering schools for the digital sector, the best AI, quantum and cyber-security experts. There is nothing complicated about it—we only need to pool our money. Do we have the money? The next budget of the European Union is proposed at around €1 trillion. At the European Commission we have suggested a revolution in spending, setting aside €30 billion of the budget for the digital sector. The biggest spending will remain on cohesion policy and agricultural policy, but since we have proposed increased funding for digital technologies and innovation we need a slight decrease in those two budget lines. You can imagine the kind of resistance there is in the Member States.

If the Commission's proposal to increase spending in the digital sector is not accepted, then I am afraid we cannot meet our ambition. Unfortunately, the likelihood is high that Member States will cut spending on innovation.

European Commission President Ursula von der Leyen's political guidelines are very clear that Europe has to regain its digital leadership and that we have to invest in new technologies. This is best done not by centralizing things in Brussels but by federating our efforts, by doing things together.

The data that we will use in the next generation of AI algorithms does not yet exist. It will have to be generated—just as the algorithms themselves will have to be invented. We are at the beginning of this process, and I do not think it is inevitably going to be a story of doom and gloom, of Europe falling behind the giants of America and China. But if we want to avoid that inevitability, now is the time to start working—and to start working together.

Notes

1. See https://www.ecb.europa.eu/press/pressconf/2019/html/ecb.is190725~547f29c369.en.html (accessed December 12, 2019).
2. See https://www.top500.org/list/2019/11/?page=1 (accessed December 16, 2019).

CHAPTER 8

EUROPE, WHAT IS TO BE DONE? THE EU BETWEEN OLD MYTHS AND NEW CHALLENGES

SVEN SIMON

INTRODUCTION

The European Union is in a paradox. Eurostat surveys show that it is more popular than ever: two out of three Europeans have a positive opinion about the supranational organization. At the same time, in many Member States, Eurosceptic parties are winning huge numbers of votes. After the European elections in May 2019, pro-European parties have only a narrow qualified majority in the European Parliament, and in 2016 in Great Britain a majority of the turnout voted to leave the European Union.

How can we reconcile these findings? The fundamental approval of the European idea faces latent skepticism towards the existing institutions. Forty percent of Europeans are dissatisfied with democracy at European level and 47 percent believe that their vote has no influence over European decisions.[1] This finding is an alarm signal, as when citizens feel that their vote does not count in the democratic process, they turn away from this process and towards populists. The stronger alienation from the European Union gets, the more European institutions become the target of conspiracy theories and manipulated or so-called fake news.

MYTH-BASED EUROSCEPTICISM

How did we get here? I am convinced that a substantial part of the resentment about European integration is generated by traditional myths. In Germany, for years and decades we have seen the same headlines about the supposed bureaucratic monster, about the democratic deficit, about the "gravy train" at German expense. One example of the EU's supposedly rampant bureaucracy is Council Regulation (EEC) no. 1677/88, probably better known as the "cucumber regulation," which was passed in 1988 and repealed again in 2009. As with many other bureaucratization narratives, our assessment of this regulation changes when we look at how it came about.

It was absolutely not the European Commission's idea to specify the degree of curvature of cucumbers, but rather a request emanating from the industry. The standards adopted by the EU were borrowed from the Danish Vegetables Act of 1926.[2] The wish to enact this regulation came explicitly from the trade, which claimed that such standard-shaped cucumbers could be packaged faster and compared better, counted more easily and transported more efficiently. This initially banal-sounding regulation is part of one of the European Union's most successful areas of activity: the creation of common—often technical—rules for a European Single Market. This is the only way that trade can function in a way that is efficient in resources and ultimately environmentally friendly. If 28 Member States are to conduct common, cross-border trade, they need common rules. If there were 28 different standards for each product, the development and production costs would be higher, the sales market smaller, and this would mean less choice and higher prices for consumers. In the vast majority of cases, the rules that sometimes seem to us so absurd thus concern the necessary adjustment standards that merely create the conditions for a functioning Single Market.

It is also interesting to see how vehemently the Member States resist if the European Commission wants to abolish a rule. When the cucumber regulation was to be abandoned, 16 Member States were against—more than those who wanted to drop it. It was finally abolished in 2009 thanks to the strength of the German vote, but many retailers in Germany still apply the cucumber regulation in their purchasing guidelines because the aforementioned advantages actually do exist.

Another example of the delegitimizing effect of Euro-myths was the announcement in summer 2019 that the EU wanted to ban sports pitches made of artificial turf. When this happened, as a Member of the European Parliament, I received many letters from the public, some concerned, some angry. What had happened? The European Commission had asked the European Chemicals Agency to compile a list of sources of microplastics. According to a study by the University of Vienna, each of us consumes a credit-card-sized amount of microplastics every week without being aware of the long-term health consequences.[3]

The avoidance of microplastics is thus a very important topic on the European regulatory agenda.

A study by the Fraunhofer Institute has shown that rubber granulate in artificial turf is one of the five most common sources of microplastic emissions in Germany.[4] Out of this story, some German newspapers created the fear-inducing headline that the EU wants to ban artificial turf. But this demand was never made, especially since now some doubts have arisen about the study's findings.[5] Rather, at the time of the outraged media reports, we were still at the very beginning of a regulatory process, during which the facts are first of all being established. If suspicions concerning rubber granulate are confirmed, we can assume that what will be discussed, if at all, is just replacing the rubber with cork infill, while taking into account the appropriate transition periods and financial support for sports clubs.

These two examples show how easily fears can be fueled by EU-related issues. Euro-myths run the risk of becoming unchallenged truth at some point through constant repetition. Sooner or later, supposedly crazy bureaucracy becomes a rhetorical sure-fire success, on which Eurosceptic parties can all too easily capitalize.

Moreover, in debates about cucumbers, light bulbs, artificial turf, and copyright, I am always amazed to see how individual questions of regulation are used to deny the legitimacy of the EU as a whole. Rules are drawn up by political majorities and these majorities can be voted out or changed through the democratic process, which is albeit more tricky at European level than in the Member States. Hardly anyone would think of demanding the abolition of the Federal Government or the Federal Republic of Germany because of a misguided turnaround in energy policy. In European debates, the inhibition threshold for such basic questions seems to be very low. That too, I am convinced, damages the European Union's resilience to crises and the ability to debate political issues in a way that leads to solutions.

When Eurosceptics say that each country should decide for themselves which rules to apply, they are indirectly calling for the abolition of the Single Market, which derives its economic added value from the fact that common standards enable fair internal competition and economies of scale. In case of doubt, 28 individual national standards would lead to 28 different versions of the same product. Therefore, it is not just sensible, but indispensable that the EU produces detailed regulations in the case of apparent questions of detail concerning the Single Market as well.

Myth-based Euroscepticism and the associated lack of support for structural reforms make it difficult for Europe to face new challenges. I am not saying that the European Union is a perfect, flawless institution. We urgently need change, especially since the world we live in is changing so fundamentally.

CHALLENGES

The West has shaped the course of world history for over 300 years—for better and for worse. It began with colonization, then came globalization: global economic standards, the overwhelming majority of international institutions and organizations, the system of international law, and the dominant understanding of human rights all originate in Europe and North America.

This western hegemony experienced a brief renaissance in the history of ideas when, after the collapse of the Soviet Union, many came to believe this was the "end of history," as the American sociologist Francis Fukuyama put it.[6] Since then, however, we have found that the economic growth of other countries with fundamentally different values—as can be seen in the People's Republic of China—leads to a remapping of global influence.

Demography also plays a central role in this. While almost every fourth inhabitant of the world was European in 1900, the proportion of our continent's population has fallen to just under 10 percent today. According to United Nations' estimates, this percentage is expected to decrease further to 7 percent by 2050.[7] There now exist neighborhoods in Beijing or Shanghai with more inhabitants than Denmark or Norway.

Economically too, Europe faces the challenge of securing its place on the world stage. Today, 90 percent of global economic growth takes place outside the European Union.[8] The pioneering digital sector seems to be permanently shared between Google, Apple, Facebook, Amazon in the West, and Samsung, Huawei, Tencent, and Alibaba in the East. Europe and Germany may lament that we have no means of resisting these oligopolies, but politics has seen recent years go by without any initiatives being implemented. Within the EU, the problems ensuing from the 2009 global economic crisis still persist. After ten years of crisis, large parts of Southern Europe still lack economic prospects. An absence of political solutions to the migration crisis exacerbates existing social tensions and identity conflicts—even in the prosperous areas of Western and Northern Europe.

What should the European Union do in the face of these diverse challenges? I am convinced that we are faced with a fundamental decision: should we give up our ability to shape the world and accept that in the future global political decisions will be taken over our heads in Washington, New Delhi, and Beijing, and that Trump, Modi, and Xi will determine our future? Or do we as Europeans want to continue to take our place on the world stage and have a say in such decisions?

If we choose the latter, we must as a consequence enable the EU to become capable of acting once more, since the European Union is the only realistic body through which we can address global challenges. To have an EU that is able to act, we need reforms in four policy areas:

1. GUARANTEED PROSPERITY

The legitimacy of a united Europe depends not least on its ability to give citizens an economic future. This applies in Frankfurt just as much as in Athens or Lisbon. The mechanism that guarantees this is free and rules-based trade. In a changing world, it is important that Europe can help shape the rules of globalization according to its own standards. In this respect, the trade agreements currently under discussion with Mercosur and Vietnam act as models, because these contracts not only regulate the reduction of customs duties, but they also oblige all contracting parties to comply with European standards in the production of goods, in environmental protection, and in handling European citizens' personal data.

In addition, the EU should at last follow the lead of Asia and the USA in terms of digitalization. For years we have been hearing that there should be European initiatives in this area—with little impact thus far in terms of realpolitik. An obvious deficiency lies in the inadequate infrastructure. Many Germans know from their own experience that even in 2019 it was still impossible to maintain cell phone reception and LTE data connectivity on the freeways and trains in the Rhein-Main area. If we want to compete seriously with countries like South Korea, such a situation is unacceptable. It is not just a problem of actual implementation in this area, but the goals themselves are dramatically unambitious too.

However, it is not just a question of remedying defects in the digital infrastructure. In my opinion, this topic can also be seen as a regulatory problem. There is still no real European digital Single Market. Each country has its own hardware infrastructure and network providers. As a result, the quality of digital services varies massively within the EU—and Germany is very rarely even average.

I recognize the problems associated with the introduction of a digital tax for a country with high exports, but I think that fair taxation of American digital companies in competition with German and European medium-sized companies is imperative. It is completely unacceptable that the average tax burden for manufacturing companies in the EU is 23 percent and for digital companies just 9 percent.

In view of the numerous and ongoing violations of European data protection and competition law by Facebook, Google, and co., we should also seriously consider unbundling these companies using antitrust law. Compared with any possible industrial policy initiatives that have, with the exception of Airbus, so far always failed, this would be the most effective way of promoting European digital companies of significant size.

In addition, Europe should structurally strengthen its competitiveness through less consumption and more investment. It is embarrassing that the city of Shanghai alone invests significantly more in AI research than the Federal Republic of Germany. Here, too, a joint billion-dollar EU investment project would be the only realistic entity that could keep up with China and the USA over the long term.

2. CLIMATE AND ENERGY UNION

Climate change is a challenge for our generation, and it should now be possible to assume that everyone is aware of the potentially catastrophic consequences. The prime question is therefore not *whether* but *how* we limit global warming to well below two degrees Celsius.

What is the best mechanism to do this? "Emissions must have a price that changes our behavior."[10] I strongly support this statement taken from Ursula von der Leyen's speech as candidate for President of the Commission. It is a basic principle of a market economy that externalities have to be priced in. However, this is currently only happening inadequately and is limited to just a few industries. A CO_2 tax is problematic in this regard, because *de facto* it sets a fixed price for emissions and thus overrides market mechanisms. Price determination, especially of externalities, creates the right incentives when the market decides on prices through supply and demand. That is why I consider the introduction of CO_2 budgets and a universalization, i.e. a comprehensive expansion of certificate trading, to be more meaningful. A fixed price in the form of a tax or a fixed certificate law only leads to a structural shortage or surplus of pollution rights in the long term, with correspondingly negative consequences for the environment or the economy.

However, we must also be aware that Europe cannot save the world on its own. Less than a fifth of all global emissions come from the EU, with the German proportion at just under 2 percent. Accordingly, the success of our climate and energy policies will depend on whether we succeed in inspiring other countries to copy them. That is why only an innovation-driven climate policy will be successful. If, on the other hand, it is conceived as a policy of de-industrialization, no emerging country will follow us along this route.

3. DEVELOPMENT OF THE COMMON SECURITY AND DEFENSE POLICY

Since the Lisbon Treaty, the Common Security and Defense Policy (CSDP) has enabled the European Union to take joint responsibility for the security of Member States in the form of a military alliance. Our immediate vicinity is today more unstable than at any time since the end of the Yugoslav wars. On the other side of the Mediterranean, Libya and Syria are failing states, there is an autocrat in charge on the Bosphorus, and our relations with Russia are at an all-time low after the annexation of Crimea, which contravened international law. In addition, we can no longer rely on our traditional security partner, the United States, to the extent that would have been a matter of course a few years ago.

Accordingly, Europe must be able to take more responsibility for its own security. But can it currently do that? The Bundeswehr is currently not a model example, to put it mildly. At the same time, most EU countries, above all Germany, still have extremely redundant structures. We have at least 28 national procurement systems, 28 personnel offices, 28 training centers, etc. If we combined them, we could not only save billions of Euros in tax revenue, but also achieve a high degree of compatibility and interoperability at the same time.

That is why last year the Permanent and Structured Cooperation (PESCO) was mobilized as a step towards a defense union. However, given the tensions in our vicinity, Europe should become more ambitious. There is still no roadmap for the creation of a European Defense Community (EDC) as once envisaged by the founding fathers of a united Europe. Only with the EDC will we be in a position to protect our Union independently.

The EU should also have the ability to act when it comes to foreign policy. But here too, the principle of unanimity and the veto power of a single Member State are currently slowing down the necessary progress. Imagine, in this instance, that all of Germany's Minister Presidents from Markus Söder to Bodo Ramelow must always agree in the Bundesrat—what would the Federal Republic's ability to act be like then? It is therefore clear that the principle of unanimity on foreign and security policy issues should be abolished if we want the European Union to be taken seriously as an actor on the world stage.

4. BUILDING A EUROPEAN PUBLIC SPHERE

Alongside the major issues of economy, climate, and security, there is also a fourth theme that forms a kind of meta-topic for the success of everything else: the need for fundamental institutional reform in Europe. We will not reach a Europe-wide consensus or compromise in any of the areas described above if we lack the forums to discuss political ideas with one another.

Ultimately, significant cultural differences exist—especially in terms of legal culture. Germany has a "parliamentary army," a system that seems indispensable in Germany, not least because of its historical experience (even if it is only based on the case law of the Federal Constitutional Court). In France, by contrast, defense is traditionally an executive power and lies in the hands of the president. What would a joint European army look like?

So far, we have lacked a common European platform for debating such issues in the public sphere. In Germany, public service broadcasts present the German perspective, while French television speaks from a French point of view. Projects such as Arte are a good start in this respect, but they operate in more of a niche way. I therefore advocate the creation of a European public "broadcasting service" that is devoted to the creation of a pan-European public sphere.

Institutional reforms can also help to build a shared public sphere. We have to strengthen Parliament as a representative body and the direct voice of European citizens. Today, only the EU Commission has the right to introduce laws, the so-called right of initiative (Art. 294 TFEU). A reform of the European treaties and a strengthening of the parliamentary system in Europe are needed here. Specifically, Parliament must not only be granted the right of initiative, but also an ongoing political supervisory function over the Commission. The lack of responsiveness in the European system is no longer appropriate to the degree of integration. The difficulty of changing primary law, which often has a constitutional status, should also be reconsidered, just as there is an urgent need for a fundamental reform of the culture of debate within the European Parliament, without which public visibility is impossible.

In debates about the future of the EU we hear all too often that these ideas are too big and that Europe cannot be reformed in any case. I think this notion is wrong and dangerous. European unification has always been a project of political will and of overcoming small-mindedness and resistance. It was by no means easy for the founding fathers of our European community of states to extend the hand of reconciliation to Germany just a few years after the end of World War II.

At a time when the ruins of war dominated the streets of many cities, and millions of families had to struggle with the painful loss of a close relative, the historic will of the generation of Adenauer and De Gaulle needed to build a shared European home. Against the backdrop of the fundamental challenges of today, we Europeans are called upon to reflect on this courage and this willingness to make decisions.

However, Europe cannot live in paper treaties or in the chambers of institutions, but rather in the hearts and minds of its citizens. Therefore, this essay is not just a commentary by a professor and a politician on the current situation—it's a direct invitation to you, dear reader, to stand up for the unity of Europe. It is our decision whether to overcome the old myths and meet the current challenges. It is our decision whether to make the European Union sustainable through its economic, environmental, and security policy, and whether we Europeans altogether are able to act. The future of Europe is in our hands.

Notes

1. European Parliament, *Parlemeter 2018*, https://www.europarl.europa.eu/at-your-service/files/be-heard/eurobarometer/2018/parlemeter-2018/report/en-parlemeter-2018.pdf (accessed December 5, 2019).

2. Jasper von Altenbockum, "Das Geheimnis der gekrümmten Gurke," 2016, https://www.faz.net/aktuell/politik/harte-bretter/brexit-kampagne-geheimnis-der-gekruemmten-gurken-14303914.html (accessed December 5, 2019).

3. *Die Welt*, "Jeder von uns isst eine Kreditkarte pro Woche," 2019, https://www.welt.de/gesundheit/article195127017/

Mikroplastik-Jeder-von-uns-isst-eine-Kreditkarte-pro-Woche.html (accessed December 5, 2019).

4. Fraunhofer Institut, *Kunststoffe in der Umwelt: Mikro- und Makroplastik*, 2018, https://www.umsicht.fraunhofer.de/content/dam/umsicht/de/dokumente/publikationen/2018/kunststoffe-id-umwelt-konsortialstudie-mikroplastik.pdf (accessed December 5, 2019).

5. Michael Fröhlingsdorf, "Forscher ziehen eigene Mikroplastik-Studie in Zweifel," 2019, https://www.spiegel.de/wissenschaft/natur/fraunhofer-institut-relativiert-studie-ueber-mikroplastik-a-1280225.html (accessed December 5, 2019).

6. Francis Fukuyama, *The End of History and the Last Man* (New York: Free Press, 1992).

7. United Nations, *World Population Prospects 2019*, https://population.un.org/wpp/ (accessed December 5, 2019).

8. European Parliament, 2016, https://www.europarl.europa.eu/doceo/document/E-8-2015-014997-ASW_EN.html?redirect (accessed December 5, 2019).

9. ifo Institut, *Die Besteuerung der Digitalwirtschaft*, 2018, https://www.ifo.de/DocDL/Studie-Digitalsteuer-2018.pdf (accessed December 5, 2019).

10. Ursula von der Leyen, https://ec.europa.eu/commission/presscorner/detail/en/SPEECH_19_4230 (accessed December 5, 2019).

CHAPTER 9

NATO AND EUROPE'S STRATEGIC AUTONOMY

KAI A. KONRAD

At the 2019 Munich Security Conference, US Vice President Michael Pence reiterated the United States' demands for increased spending by its European allies, saying:

> The truth is, many of our NATO Allies still need to do more. And the United States expects every NATO member to put in place a credible plan to meet the 2 percent threshold. And, by 2024, we expect all our allies to invest 20 percent of defense spending on procurement.[1]

Let's look at the numbers.[2] In 2017 US defense spending was approximately $643 billion by comparison with approximately $56 billion in the United Kingdom, $46 billion in France, and $46 billion in Germany. The differences are striking when we look at this expenditure as a proportion of the countries' gross domestic products. While it is expected that the United States spent 3.42 percent of GDP in 2019, in most of the other countries it is more or less well below 2 percent of GDP. In many cases, the smaller the country, the lower the percentage. According to the NATO press release, the Grand Duchy of Luxembourg is expected to spend as little as 0.55 percent of its GDP on defense in 2019, that is a total of $391 million.

What conclusions can we draw from these figures? Is Europe once again under US protection? How serious is the US demand, and how credible is the statement by US Secretary of Defense Mattis that the United States will modify its own commitment if things do not change?[3]

If we look at the past 50 years, we can see that asymmetry in the spending of the United States and its allies is not a new state of affairs. A famous study by Mancur Olson and Richard Zeckhauser shows that in the past the United States spent about 9 percent of its economic resources on defense, compared with

5.5 percent in Germany, 6.7 percent in France, and 7 percent in the United Kingdom. In the Grand Duchy of Luxembourg it was 1.7 percent.[4]

Across all NATO countries, arms spending has declined in relation to each country's economic resources. This is a peace dividend that emerged out of the end of the Cold War. However, the relative proportions have changed only minimally: the major countries pay disproportionately large amounts relative to their economic resources, and this applies most dramatically to the largest country, the United States of America. The aforementioned NATO press release also shows that for many decades a difference has existed in the level of expenditure as a proportion of GDP between the United States on the one hand and Europe and Canada on the other, a difference that has not increased noticeably in recent times.

If such asymmetrical burden sharing has persisted over 50 years, we have to ask whether there are not significant natural causes for the invariance of this structural asymmetry in NATO's budget. What incentive does a small country such as Luxembourg have to contribute several million to NATO's defense efforts? Does such an amount really make a difference to Luxembourg's defense capabilities and security interests? Or would the more than 600,000 Luxembourgers not be better advised to use their military budget for things that directly and only benefit the citizens of Luxembourg, for example, to reduce the tax burden by around $650 per capita annually? Would the United States abandon its own efforts to be the independent world military power if Luxembourg completely canceled its NATO contribution? In fact, the game theory that says that in a defense alliance all succeed together or all go down together, predicts the opposite, namely that the United States will step up its efforts if it expects a decrease in the efforts of its smaller allies.[5]

Now we could say that fairness demands that everyone, even Luxembourg, should participate in NATO's defense capabilities. Donald Trump invokes fairness as part of his argument, as quoted in the *New York Times*: "NATO members must finally contribute their fair share and meet their financial obligations..."[6] In fact, however, international politics rarely operates according to the principles of fairness. More important and robust determinants are the individual countries' interests and the opportunities they have to assert their interests under existing conditions.

With the collapse of the Iron Curtain, the NATO alliance lost many of its shared collective goals. In addition, there are today growing doubts as to whether the United States would use its resources in Europe in the extreme case of undertaking a massive nuclear strike to defend individual countries on the defense alliance's Eastern European border. The United States has also developed political and military priorities in regions and in relation to states that do not have the same status for Western European members of the alliance.

In *The Economist* magazine, French President Emmanuel Macron complained about the unsatisfactory state of the cooperation between the United States and the (European) allies within the NATO alliance—possibly against the backdrop of changing interests.[7] He also advocated a European strategic independence, saying that Europe should become a geopolitical power, including in military terms. These ideas are understandable. It only makes sense to follow in the United States' slipstream in terms of defense policy if it is clear that the United States will ultimately use its military resources to pursue Europe's goals as well.

If interests within a military alliance correspond, and the benefits from the defense capability flow automatically to all allies as a collective good, as was perhaps the case when defending the Western community of values against threats posed by the Warsaw Pact, the smaller allies are in a highly satisfactory position. The logic of game theory says that the dominant ally cannot help but act "benevolently," making the dominant defense contribution out of pure self-interest.

In a world where a hegemonic power defines the goals of the alliance and these goals no longer correspond with the goals of the other members, the other members may focus on their own goals and pursue them independently. The distribution of advantages and disadvantages changes as shared collective goals take a back seat. In extreme cases, the hegemonic power pursues its own goals and even uses its power against its allies.

Such elements are also to be found in the relationship between the United States and the European allies, for example in the imposition of billion-dollar fines, such as those imposed on Swiss Banks by the United States in connection with tax evasion by American citizens.[8] The same applies to the enforcement of American sanctions against third countries. Companies based in alliance countries that undermine these sanctions risk being excluded from the "dollar system."[9]

In this changing environment, France's desire for European strategic independence is understandable. It remains unclear how realistic such an option is.

On the one hand, we have to ask whether Europeans can agree on a common policy. In the past, potential opportunities have not been exploited consistently.

Extensive talks between France and Germany about possible cooperation in the field of nuclear defense took place in the second half of the 1950s, were put on hold after the collapse of the Fourth Republic, and were no longer pursued by the new government under Charles de Gaulle.[10] In the 1960s, talks between the United Kingdom and France over possible nuclear deterrence cooperation also came to nothing.[11]

It is unclear whether the United States will simply allow the emancipation of its old allies to take place. A case study for this is the development of the Galileo satellite navigation system.[12] It was intended that this system operate alongside the US-controlled GPS, making Europe and the other states involved in the Galileo project independent of GPS. The United States can selectively restrict civilian use of GPS. This can happen, for example, in the event of military conflicts with non-allied regions, but equally it is not impossible technically for the United States to restrict such use for other reasons. The European project, which was launched with the founding of Galileo Industries, aimed to eliminate this dependency.

France favored a Galileo specification that also permits military applications, thus enabling military action without the approval and support of the United States. However, the development of Galileo was accompanied by considerable controversy between the Europeans and the United States. From a realpolitik point of view, Galileo threatened the US monopoly in the field of satellite-based navigation, which also applies to the use of satellite navigation for civilian use. A long negotiation process ensued that has ultimately led to a partial integration of the systems rather than the establishment of parallel, totally independent systems.

Over the coming years and decades, Europe and the United States may move closer once more. It may also be the case that the divergence of interests will continue to grow and become permanent. The current political situation and the incumbent US President clearly show the consequences that Europe's one-sided strategic dependency on the United States can have in the face of divergent interests and the contingencies of democratic electoral processes.

The US desire for increased military spending in Europe plays a key role in these considerations. The call for high capital spending in this area, as expressed in the above quotation by the US Secretary of State, may only have been meant as a call for more money to be invested in US weapons systems and armaments. This interpretation would be consistent with the view that the current international policy of the United

States is largely focused on commercial gain and is aimed at supporting US exports.

However, this demand also offers European allies the opportunity of fulfilling it by developing independent European weapon systems. It may be questionable whether the United States will allow such an initiative to happen, or whether it will intervene as it did with satellite navigation and try to prevent the development of military independence. In any case, Europe would have a lot to gain if it succeeded in taking a consistent and successful route away from strategic dependency.

Notes

1. Remarks by Vice President Pence at the 2019 Munich Security Conference, Munich, Germany, https://www.whitehouse.gov/briefings-statements/remarks-vice-president-pence-2019-munich-security-conference-munich-germany/ (accessed November 16, 2019).

2. On the figures, cf. NATO Press Release, 25 June 2019, Defence Expenditure of NATO Countries (2012–2019), COMMUNIQUEPR/CP(2019)069, https://www.nato.int/nato_static_fl2014/assets/pdf/pdf_2019_06/20190625_PR2019-069-EN.pdf (accessed November 11, 2019).

3. Helene Cooper, "Defense Secretary Mattis Tells NATO Allies to Spend More, or Else" in *New York Times*, February 15, 2017.

4. Mancur Olson and Richard Zeckhauser, "An Economic Theory of Alliances" in *Review of Economics and Statistics*, 48 (3), pp. 266–279.

5. Theodore C. Bergstrom, Lawrence Blume, and Hal Varian, "On the Private Provision of Public Goods" in *Journal of Public Economics*, 29 (1), 1986, pp. 25–49.

6. Cf. Peter Baker, "Trump Says NATO Allies Don't Pay Their Share. Is That True?" in *New York Times*, May 26, 2017, https://www.nytimes.com/2017/05/26/world/europe/nato-trump-spending.html (accessed November 16, 2019).

7. Cf. "A Continent in Peril" in *The Economist*, November 9–15, 2019, p. 9.

8. Cf. for example, Matthew Allen, "'Category 2' Swiss Banks Handed $ 1.36 bn Final Bill," 2016, https://www.swissinfo.ch/eng/tax-evasion_us-scheme-ends-with-final-1.36bn-bill-for-swiss-banks/41923378 (accessed November 16, 2019); ibid., "Credit Suisse Admits US Tax Evasion Guilt," 2014, https://www.swissinfo.ch/eng/bank-prosecuted_credit-suisse-admits-us-tax-evasion-guilt/38595532 (accessed November 16, 2019).

9. Cf. for example, Victor Mallet, "Abide by US Sanctions on Iran or Drop the Dollar, Mnuchin says" in *Financial Times*, July 18, 2019, https://www.ft.com/content/09799460-a958-11e9-984c-fac8325aaa04 (accessed November 16, 2019).

10. Cf. Peter Siebenmorgen, *Franz Josef Strauß: Ein Leben im Übermaß* (Munich: Siedler Verlag, 2015), pp. 125–147.

11. Cf. Chloe Cornish, "UK Considered Nuclear Defence Deal with France in 1960s" in *Financial Times*, July 20, 2017, https://www.ft.com/content/fc6d0980-6c7f-11e7-b9c7-15af748b60d0 (accessed November 16, 2019); Kristian Stoddart, "Nuclear Weapons in Britain's Policy Towards France, 1960–1974" in *Diplomacy and Statecraft*, 18 (4), 2007, pp. 719–744.

12. Cf. Bastian Giegerich, "Navigating Differences: Transatlantic Negotiations over Galileo" in *Cambridge Review of International Affairs*, 20 (3), 2007, pp. 491–508; ESA article, "Galileo: Europas Unabhängigkeit und Kooperation," http://www.esa.int/Space_in_Member_States/Austria/Galileo_Europas_Unabhaengigkeit_und_Kooperation (accessed November 16, 2019).

CHAPTER 10

EUROPEAN IDENTITY IN CHALLENGING TIMES: ADVOCATING THE EUROPEAN SUCCESS MODEL WITH CONFIDENCE

CLAUDIA WIESNER

What is Europe? And what is the *raison d'être*, i.e., the mission of the European Union? Today, the question of the substance of the European integration project, of a "European identity," is on everyone's lips and is often linked to the EU's current symptoms of crisis. So what does the EU stand for in the age of Brexit, the financial crisis, and competition with China and the United States? In this essay I want to examine all these questions. I will start with a conceptual clarification of the term "European identity." I will then discuss the substance—the values, policy models, policy content, and rights—for which the European Union stands. The main thesis of this essay is that the EU is, and has, a success model to advocate. This model combines economic prosperity and social equality with the values derived from Article 2 of the EU Treaty: respect for human dignity, freedom, democracy, equality, the rule of law, respect for human rights, pluralism, non-discrimination, tolerance, justice, solidarity, and the equality of women and men. In the second part of this essay, I argue that both EU representatives and EU citizens can and should advocate this "European success model" worldwide and with confidence.

1. WHAT IS THE POINT OF A EUROPEAN IDENTITY?

First of all, the term "European identity" comes with a degree of vagueness: the continent of Europe and the European Union are not identical, but in public as well as scholarly debate the two are often equated or interconnected. In this essay, I will refer to the European Union and discuss elements of an EU-related political and democratic identity. Nevertheless, historical aspects of the concept of Europe and references to the continent of Europe are of course in many ways interwoven with the EU, and even scholarly debate often talks about "European identity" when what is meant is the identity of the EU. In debates within the social and in particular the political sciences, the question of a European identity has been discussed since the 1990s in connection with the further democratization of the EU.[1]

From a normative-theoretical perspective, the democratization of the EU and the formation of European identity must be linked. This link refers to the three basic, ideal-typical dimensions of legitimate democracies, and especially to the input dimension. These three dimensions of democracy are, for instance, expressed in Abraham Lincoln's classic formula in his Gettysburg Address, where he defines democracy as "government *of* the people, *by* the people, *for* the people." These three dimensions of democracy are similarly found in a wide variety of conceptual ideas about the EU.[2]

The first is the *input dimension* of democratic life: citizens support democratic life, on the one hand as *sovereign* and as the electorate, and on the other hand through their *political activities*, i.e. by participating in debates, through protests, or by setting up the organizations of civil society. The second component of the Lincoln formula refers to the fact that democracy literally means government *by* the people. In representative democracies, this means the rights to vote and be elected, the organization of the system of representative democracy, and the relationships between citizens and governed, i.e. *representation* of the governed, *responsibility* towards the governed, and the *institutional organization* that makes this possible. The third component of the Lincoln formula emphasizes that government must take place *for* the people, that is, it concerns the *output* of the system and the *relationship* between government and governed, that is, whether citizens are satisfied with the decisions their representatives have taken on their behalf, and whether the latter can be held responsible for their decisions. The Lincoln formula thus refers to three central elements of legitimate representative democracies: the *input dimension*, the *representative or institutional* dimension, and the *output* dimension.

All three imply an important normatively grounded connection of democracy and democratic identity: a representative democratic polity, its institutions and procedures, must be supported by a democratic subject, a demos, which defines itself as such at a basic level. Democratic identity means this *self-definition of the demos*, i.e. 1) an awareness of and identification with the level at which rights and democratic practice are related, and 2) a mutual identification and recognition between the members of the demos.

Democratic identity thus relates to processes of identification that operate in two directions: first, *horizontally*, between citizens who *mutually recognize each other as members of a demos*; and second, *vertically*, from the *citizens to the level of the system and the government*, who identify with them and accept their policy outputs.

In the first place, such a democratic identity has a *functional aspect*. As David Easton says, political systems depend to a certain extent on *identification* and *support* from their citizens in order to remain stable.[3] In this sense, democratic identity is first of all a *necessary condition for stable democratic systems*. Second, resilient democratic identities enable the *acceptance of majority decisions and policies of redistribution*.[4] There is also a third, central normative argument in democratic theory: regardless of whether it is based on a republican, communitarian, or liberal model, from a normative point of view democracy must comprise not just electoral and civil rights but also democratic practice, in which democratic identity plays a key role. For example, citizens of a polity will most likely become politically active only if they have at least an *awareness* of their belonging to this polity. *Democratic identity is therefore also needed for citizens to take ownership of democratic institutions and rights*, for them to participate, mobilize, and protest. The formation of democratic identity is *both a consequence of democratic practice and its precondition.*[5]

All three functions—ensuring the stability of the system, making redistribution decisions acceptable, and enabling democratic practice—are essential for democratic identity.

2. THE DEMOCRATIC IDENTITY OF THE EU

In the last few decades, the role of the input component of democratic legitimacy and its relationship to democratic identity has been debated in Germany in particular. Various authors have emphasized that democratization of the EU's institutions alone (i.e. expanding the powers of the European Parliament, for example) is not enough, since democracy also needs a demos—and that is why the EU also needs to develop active citizenship, the public sphere, civil society, and indeed a European identity, which would form the EU's demos in the first place.[6]

However, in the argument about the processes suggested for developing an EU demos two fundamental positions are in competition, especially in the German-language debate. On the one hand, proponents of the so-called *no demos thesis* argue that the EU has no demos because it lacks the demos elements of the public sphere, civil society, and in particular European identity,[7] and that even in the future these elements are not likely to emerge. They argue that the EU therefore lacks the basis for input legitimacy and thus cannot be democratized any further.[8]

However, this argument sets up as mandatory a normative *chronological sequence* in the creation of a demos and democratization (i.e., "first create a demos, then begin democratization")—and this argument must be rejected based both on normative-theoretical grounds and empirical findings.

Although the representatives of the *no demos thesis* rightly emphasize the importance of a demos and in particular European identity, they wrongly argue that these should be in place *before* the EU can be democratized further. In so doing, they are making a *pre-political* European identity the *condition* for further democratization of the EU. This conclusion not only leads to a circular argument that must always reject the further democratization of the EU (no demos—no democratization—no democratic activity—no formation of a demos—no democratization, etc.), it also does not necessarily result from the normative-theoretical relation between identity and democracy. It leads merely to the claim that democracy needs a demos, but not to conclusions about when it should be created.

In fact, the formation of a demos is *closely related to democratic practice*. Accordingly, the proponents of the second basic position in the German debate emphasize that European identity, the public sphere, and civil society can and will most likely intensify or develop precisely through the process of democratization and the resulting democratic practice at EU level.[9]

The EU's democratic identity is thus a form of collective identity in the sense of collectively shared patterns of identification, and it is not to be compared to an individual's personal identity. The term refers to human or social collectives. In turn, a collective is a *gathering of people*; and identity conceptually refers to *equality*. The identity of human collectives therefore means that these collectives *appear to be the same, from a particular point of view* at least.[10]

"Collective identities" can therefore be found in human collectives who create their own identity, i.e., their common ground, that is they *construct them socially*. Collective identities are characterized by a) *collective patterns of identity* or collectively shared orientations of individual identifications or attitudes, and b) their *substance*, namely particular patterns of meaning as macro-phenomena overarching individual identifications. Collective identities are "imagined communities."[11] So democratic identity of the EU means that Members of the EU demos are aware that they constitute this demos.

3. WHAT DOES THE EU STAND FOR?

Eurobarometer's quantitative surveys over the past decades show that EU citizens' awareness about the EU has grown, and more than half of the EU's citizens feel that they are EU citizens.[12] On this issue, we may rightly ask whether the glass is half full or half empty, i.e. whether that is enough. I argue that it is enough—especially if we compare the situation with the one in Germany after the foundation of the German Empire. In 1872, if you had asked Bavarians and Prussians whether they felt German and recognized each other as members of a demos, I doubt that the figures would have exceeded 50 percent.

The crucial challenge to the EU's democratic identity is a different one. It concerns the second component of collective identity: it is unclear what citizens identify with when they identify with the EU. As we saw at the beginning, it is unclear what the EU stands for. The EU does not currently have a grand narrative that connects people to it. But what might connect people with the EU?

My argument is that the EU can show a number of successes that it should advocate more powerfully, on the basis of which it can act confidently in the world, and which can also strengthen the EU internally—if they are actively implemented, i.e. can also be substantiated with real policies. The EU stands for:

- peaceful cooperation and multilateralism
- democracy
- the rule of law
- human rights
- civil rights
- equal treatment and non-discrimination
- economic strength and economic success
- a social market economy and a well-developed welfare state
- sustainability

These dimensions stand for what I suggest to term a "European success model" that is unparalleled in the world. It is precisely these European values that the world needs.

Jean-Claude Juncker, who bowed out as President of the European Commission at the end of 2019, already put this model into words in a 2005 speech on the Lisbon Strategy:

> What do the citizens of Europe want? Competitiveness? Yes. Higher growth? Yes. Higher productivity? Yes. But these terms do not speak to their hearts. [...] What Europeans really want, in fact, is work. They want to be able to set up their company in good conditions and find the finance for it and they want open markets and efficient communications and transport systems. They want to be able to reconcile their family life with their professional life and keep up with the new technologies and the world of the Internet. They want a good education for their children, public utility services, decent pensions and a healthy environment.[13]

Alongside these output-oriented goals, the European Union also stands for certain democratic values. Here I understand values to be fundamental, normative principles that structure the law and political action—one might also call them constitutional principles. They are therefore neither "goals" nor "strategy." In the EU, these values are put down in the treaties, even if they build on the historical and cultural heritage of the continent,[14] which is also described in the present book, as well as on the rule of law and democratic traditions of the Member States.

The EU has endorsed these values and developed them along similar lines. After it had been primarily an economic community for a long time (1952–93), the EU's political values were formulated more precisely and in more detail with the 1993 Maastricht Treaty and the founding of the EU.

Today, Article 2 of the Treaty on European Union states:

> The Union is founded on the values of respect for human dignity, freedom, democracy, equality, the rule of law and respect for human rights, including the rights of persons belonging to minorities. These values are common to the Member States in a society in which pluralism, non-discrimination, tolerance, justice, solidarity and equality between women and men prevail.[15]

Article 49 of the Treaty on European Union makes it a condition for the admission of states to the EU that they respect these values and are committed to their promotion.[16]

The EU also has a Charter of Fundamental Rights, which defines a basic catalog of human rights, civil rights, freedoms, rights on equality and solidarity, and judicial rights.

4. CHALLENGES TO EUROPEAN VALUES

In today's EU, however, this substance of a democratic identity faces significant challenges. First, in the case of the legally enshrined values described above in particular, the crux lies in their implementation, for example in countries such as Poland, Hungary, and Romania. Hungary has been described by Prime Minister Orban himself as an "illiberal democracy." Orban does not want to adhere to the basic principles of the rule of law, which follow from the EU's already sparse catalog, and has significantly curtailed press freedom, among other things. In Poland, laws concerning the choice of judges have been changed, corruption was rampant in Romania—the list could go on and extend to other Member States.

However, democracy is not a vocabulary that can be freely interpreted: there are minimum standards that democracies must adhere to, and these include the separation of powers (Poland, Hungary) and freedom of the press.

The EU has an instrument to sanction non-compliance with minimum democratic standards—the so-called "Article 7 Procedure."

Article 7 of the EU Treaty states:

> 2. The European Council, acting by unanimity on a proposal by one third of the Member States or by the Commission and after obtaining the consent of the European Parliament, may determine the existence of a serious and persistent breach by a Member State of the values referred to in Article 2, after inviting the Member State in question to submit its observations.
>
> 3. Where a determination under paragraph 2 has been made, the Council, acting by a qualified majority, may decide to suspend certain of the rights deriving from the application of the Treaties to the Member State in question, including the voting rights of the representative of the government of that Member State in the Council. In doing so, the Council shall take into account the possible consequences of such a suspension on the rights and obligations of natural and legal persons.[17]

Such proceedings were launched against Poland, but have now stalled. So far, the Council has not secured a majority in favor of proceedings against Hungary. The Article 7 procedure is therefore difficult to implement and enforce. It is not a completely toothless tiger, but it is a rather weak tiger with few teeth.

However, if the EU allows its values to be eroded internally, it will undermine its own basis—the fundamental democratic values of the EU must therefore be made binding on all Member States, and stronger instruments of control and enforcement are needed, applied to all Member States.

In addition to these conflicts over the values of the EU, there are yet more internal and external challenges. There is currently an internal crisis in the EU in various respects—especially with regard to Brexit, but also in the debate about migration policy. Moreover, the European Parliament as well as EU governments contain fewer committed Europhiles, and EU critics and right-wing populists are gaining political influence and weight. Externally, there are numerous fundamental questions. I would like to give two examples: in the Mediterranean, how should and can the EU act in such a way that does justice to its humanitarian values and the principle of human dignity? How should it position itself in the face of geopolitical and economic competitors such as China, Russia, and the USA?

5. ADVOCATING THE EUROPEAN SUCCESS MODEL WITH CONFIDENCE

These problems do not relativize the "European success model" I have described, but they do require us to reflect on it and on how it can be strengthened internally and externally.

The EU should be strengthened internally. This also includes clearly defining and enforcing common values. In other words, not only politicians, but also we citizens have to clarify our unresolved questions and conflicts of values internally. We also have to debate what the EU stands for, what the EU's common good is or should be. We can then convey this to the outside world and advocate it confidently. The "European success model" is very attractive—if it works and is advocated with conviction.

A functioning "European success model" will also strengthen the democratic identity of the EU as a collective identity because citizens will identify with it.

This means that:

• The EU should become a subject of debate. We should not be afraid to ask and say—whether as academics, politicians, business representatives, or citizens—what kind of EU we want, and what kind of substance the

EU should stand for. This is the only way to reach agreement on how the EU defines itself internally in terms of democracy and diversity.

- We also have to democratize the EU. The EU represents democratic values—it should not be afraid of democracy. Debating, democratizing, politicizing, and also de-nationalizing (to some extent) are the relevant keywords. The EU must reduce the role of experts, increase legitimacy and transparency, carry its citizens along with it, and take their fears into account. In so doing, the "European success model" could build on the experience of the German "social market economy"— and expand it into a sustainable market economy with global responsibility.

- The EU should advocate its values to the outside world more actively. It could act as a pioneer of global regulation, social and occupational safety standards, and the protection of human rights and the environment more powerfully than hitherto, and could play a pioneering role in global democratization. This also includes the implementation of clear standards—and the designation of boundaries—in the face of economic, geopolitical, and political competitors such as the USA, China, Brazil, and Russia. However, this furthermore entails a strategy of promoting democracy towards local residents and in development policy.

In this way, the "European success model" can be strengthened and can clarify the substance associated with it—I have comprehensively shown that this substance already exists. The substance and values are important in themselves, but they are also useful. Of course market economies can work without democracy, but democracies are generally more prosperous and stable. The world needs European values.

Notes

1. For a more comprehensive version of the following arguments, see Claudia Wiesner, *Demokratisierung der EU durch nationale Europadiskurse? Strukturen und Prozesse europäischer Identitätsbildung im deutsch-französischen Vergleich* (Baden-Baden: Nomos, 2014); Ibid., "Was ist europäische Identität? Theoretische Zugänge, empirische Befunde, Forschungsperspektiven und Arbeitsdefinition" in Gudrun Hentges, Hans-Wolfgang Platzer, and Kristina Nottbohm (eds.), *Europäische Identität in der Krise? Europäische Identitätsforschung und Rechtspopulismusforschung im Dialog* (Wiesbaden: Springer, 2017), pp. 21–56.

2. See for example Jürgen Habermas, "Euroskepsis, Markteuropa, oder Europa der (Welt-)Bürger" in *Zeit der Übergänge* (Frankfurt am Main: Suhrkamp, 2001), pp. 85–103; Fritz W. Scharpf, "Legitimacy in the Multilevel

European Polity" in *European Political Science Review* 1 (2009), pp. 173–204.

3. See for example David Easton, "A Re-assessment of the Concept of Political Support" in *British Journal of Political Science* 5 (1975), pp. 435–457.

4. See Easton, "A Re-assessment"; Jürgen Habermas, "Is the Development of a European Identity Necessary, and Is It Possible?" in *The Divided West* (Cambridge: Polity, 2006), pp. 67–83; Fritz W. Scharpf, "Demokratische Politik in der internationalisierten Ökonomie" in Michael T. Greven (ed.), *Demokratie – eine Kultur des Westens?* (Opladen: Leske + Budrich, 1998), pp. 81–103.

5. Cf. Michael T. Greven, "Mitgliedschaft, Grenzen und politischer Raum: Problemdimension der Demokratisierung der Europäischen Union" in Beate Kohler-Koch (ed.), *Regieren in entgrenzten* Räumen (Opladen: Leske + Budrich, 1998) pp. 249–270, p. 253 ff.; Habermas, "Is the Development of a European Identity Necessary," pp. 76 ff.

6. Jürgen Habermas, "Remarks on Dieter Grimm's 'Does Europe Need a Constitution?'" in *European Law Journal* vol. 1, no. 3, November 1995, pp. 303–307; Peter Graf Kielmannsegg, "Integration und Demokratie" in Markus Jachtenfuchs and Beate Kohler-Koch (eds.), *Europäische Integration* (Opladen: Leske + Budrich, 1996, pp. 47–71; Scharpf, "Demokratische Politik."

7. Josef H. H. Weiler, "Der Staat 'über alles' – Demos, Telos und die Maastricht-Entscheidung des Bundesverfassungsgerichts" 1995, p. 4. https://jeanmonnetprogram.org/archive/papers/95/9507ind.html (accessed March 5, 2020).

8. For example, Kielmannsegg "Integration und Demokratie"; Peter Graf Kielmannsegg, "Integration und Demokratie" in Markus Jachtenfuchs and Beate Kohler-Koch (eds.), Europäische Integration, 2nd edn. (Opladen: Leske + Budrich 2003), pp. 49–83; Scharpf, "Demokratische Politik."

9. For example, Habermas, "Remarks on Dieter Grimm's 'Does Europe Need a Constitution?'" pp. 190 f; M. Rainer Lepsius, "Die europäische Union. Ökonomisch-politische Integration und kulturelle Pluralität" in Rien T. Segers and Reinhold Viehoff (eds.), *Kultur, Identität, Europa. Über die Schwierigkeiten und Möglichkeiten einer Konstruktion* (Frankfurt am Main: Suhrkamp, 1999), pp. 201–222.

10. Lutz Niethammer, *Kollektive Identität. Heimliche Quellen einer unheimlichen Konjunktur* (Hamburg: Rowohlt Taschenbuch, 2000), pp. 9 ff.

11. Or "imagined political communities" as Benedict Anderson wrote: Benedict Anderson, *Imagined Communities. Reflections on the Origin and Spread of Nationalism* (London: Verso, 2006), p. 6.

12. For further details, see Wiesner, *Demokratisierung der EU durch nationale Europadiskurse?* and Wiesner "Was ist europäische Identität?"

13. Jean-Claude Juncker, "Jean-Claude Juncker sur la stratégie de Lisbonne," 2005, http://www.eu2005.lu/fr/actualites/communiques/2005/03/23conseurlis/index.html (accessed November 27, 2019).

14. Claudia Wiesner and Meike Schmidt-Gleim (eds.), *The Meanings of Europe* (London: Routledge, 2014).

15. European Union, Lisbon Treaty: Consolidated Version of the Treaty on the Functioning of the European Union, 2012. https://eur-lex.europa.eu/LexUriServ/LexUriServ.do?uri=CELEX:12012E/TXT:en:PDF (accessed February 6, 2020).

16. Ibid.

17. Ibid.

CHAPTER 11

NEW VIEWS OF FAMILIAR TERRAIN

HANS ULRICH OBRIST AND EDI RAMA
IN CONVERSATION

An edited transcript of a conversation between Hans Ulrich Obrist and Edi Rama at the Convoco Forum on July 27, 2019 in Salzburg

Hans Ulrich Obrist: It's wonderful to be back at Convoco! As always, Corinne and I discussed over the course of the year which artist to involve in the Forum. In the 1960s, artists John Latham and Barbara Steveni, who founded the Artist Placement Group, had the radical idea that every organization, government, and corporation should always have an artist-in-residence or on the board. This, we believe, is still a very good idea.

The other day, I found an old conversation I had with the late Umberto Eco, the visionary Italian writer, in which he talked about that very idea in relation to Europe. He remembered having been invited to the European Union together with Rem Koolhaas and others to think about what art, architecture, and poetry could do at the core of the EU. The late Umberto Eco said we should never forget this idea.

This year, we thought it would be fascinating to invite an artist who is also a politician. Edi Rama's art and his politics basically go together. He is the Prime Minister of Albania (since 2013); he is the former Mayor of Tirana (from 2000 to 2011); and he has produced an artistic language to generate a platform for discussion and exchange. The artist as political activist intervening in societal structures brings to mind of course Joseph Beuys. It's interesting that Rama, who actually trained as a painter, has from the very beginning been interested in ideas about art's role in society.

Edi has also been very outspoken about the importance of Europe. In an article in *The Guardian*, he was quoted saying that membership of the EU would mean finally placing Albania "in a safe zone from the curse of history." That connects to something Jürgen Habermas said when he called for the European project to realize its democratic potential by evolving into a cosmopolitan community. What he means is a cross-border awareness of a shared destiny, or what we could call in German a "grenzüberschreitende Willensbildung," to quote Habermas.

Edi, we met through our friend Anri Sala, the amazing artist and filmmaker. Anri told me this story that when he was in his early teens, growing up in Tirana, he once came home and told his parents that they should let him be an artist. You were his mentor, and he told me that, for you, it all started with painting. So, I wanted to ask you to tell us a bit about that and about your beginnings as an artist.

Edi Rama: Thank you for having me here. I hope that after the heavy stuff you heard all day, maybe we can provide a lighter end. Yeah, I'm the Prime Minister of Albania and for around 20 years now have been in politics. But art has been my reason for being ever since I was a kid. I continue to do it—I just do it in my office now. It's serious; it's not something to laugh about.

Of course, being born in Communist Albania and having to deal with art was not a simple exercise, because at that time Albania was the North Korea of

Europe. We were separated totally not only from the degenerate West, but also from the treacherous East. Our art was very much limited to Socialist Realism. We grew up in a country where the art and culture of the 20th century were literally banned, where Gustav Mahler, for example, was banned, where Marcel Proust, of course, was banned, and where the teaching of art at the Academy of Arts in the late 1980s ended with Gustave Courbet.

After Courbet, we had four lectures without slides and with a depressed professor telling us how terrible things turned out because of some spoilt petit-bourgeois kids called Impressionists; and then because of a psychopath called Vincent van Gogh; and then because of an antisocial type called Paul Gauguin; and then because of the devil in person called Pablo Picasso. But this was all not visual, and to get access to the images was really difficult and also dangerous. Albania was a country where many things happened that today no one would believe.

HUO: It was in 1999 that I met the then very young Anri Sala for the first time. At the time, he was still studying at the art school Le Fresnoy in France and told me how you had convinced his skeptical parents to let him be an artist. He also told me the story that the year before, in 1998, when your father had died from a heart attack, you came back for the funeral, never left Tirana again, and soon after became Minister of Culture. Can you tell us a bit about this entry into politics from art?

ER: I went back to Tirana to bury my father, and after the funeral, I became Minister of Culture. This episode shows that it's not always easy to understand the place I live in. It's something that I need more time to explain, but it came about because during the change of the regime, everything started in the Academy of Arts. As in the other former Communist countries, the Albanian anti-regime movements started from the arts by taking what was at the time a very brave step, namely, to show in public images that were forbidden and to open up those chapters of the history of art that were banned.

Romania was the last country to cede from the former Soviet empire. Albania had been disconnected from the block since 1960 because it had wanted to be loyal to Stalin. It then took one year, from 1989 to 1990. During that year, in the Academy of Arts, things moved and created an environment from which everything blew up. The day of the blow-up was the tenth anniversary of the death of John Lennon, which provided a reason for having the first music party in a public space, where people could share forbidden music and some alcohol. The build-up of one year and Lennon's *Power to the People* song together made up the cocktail that then unleashed the movement. After this, I then continued to live in a kind of schizophrenia between art and politics, not as a politician, but as a citizen. So, somehow, I became a professional troublemaker.

At that moment in 1998, I was given the Minister of Culture job without ever having thought of becoming a Minister. The Ministry of Culture was the first public state building I ever entered.

HUO: Of course, we want to talk more about politics, but I want to ask one last question about this early period of art-making, because then you became Mayor of Tirana and that led to an extraordinary project in which you decided to basically bring hope to the city through colors. It would be interesting to hear a bit about this project through which you brought art into society.

ER: As I said previously, Albania was the North Korea of Europe, a very heavily collectivistic society, in which no private property of any sort was allowed, and in which even God was prohibited. Among all the Communist countries of Europe, Albania was the only country that was under the spell of the Chinese Cultural Revolution. When the regime disconnected from the Soviet Union and its satellites, our new love story was with China. We had songs about Albania and China being the two lions that preserve the species.

When the regime collapsed, people started to search for their own identity. Under the spell of the Chinese Cultural Revolution, we had been obliged to have the same type of haircut and to wear the same type of dress. It was even prescribed how wide the pants could be so as to not look like the Beatles: it was 24 centimeters. I'm not kidding. I remember times when we would go to the beach, we would get off the train, and there were people with scissors who would check the pants, and if the pants were too large—swish! Then the consequences were terrible.

After the regime change, people were eager to recuperate their own individual identity through private property. This was very disruptive because people started to move: People from the cities left to go to Italy and to other parts of Europe, while people from the peripheries moved to the cities. As a result, every park, every square meter of public space was occupied. First, people were putting tables on the streets and selling things. Then they were building kiosks and eventually entire buildings. When I became Mayor, Tirana was a city without public space.

There was a big run to bring the world into the house—the television, the fridge, the washing machine. By the way, TV sets at that time were allowed only by authorization, and there were boards in institutions that decided whom to authorize. In Tirana, the streets were full of thrown-away packaging materials.

At the same time, from within the buildings, people were trying to get more space. So, balconies were transformed into additional kitchen space. Ground-floor windows were turned into doors, the bedroom became a flower shop, and the living room was transformed into a bar. People on the top floors broke through the roof to add more space, because at that time we lived in very tight spaces.

Instead of social housing, the regime had built 600,000 bunkers to protect Albania from the hypothetical attack of the American imperialists. The cost of a bunker was the cost of an apartment of 75 square meters. Imagine if they had built apartments instead of bunkers.

This was the situation when I became Mayor. Nobody cared anymore about the outside. The buildings looked like a kind of popular de-constructivism. There was not one architect, but everyone was pushing from behind the walls. It was terrible, gray, disruptive. What to do with a budget that was nothing-point-something and with people who had big expectations?

So, we started by painting the buildings. It came out of necessity. Many times this has been wrongly described as an aesthetic operation. But it was a political operation with colors.

We took our oaths and started to paint. It was incredible because the money we used came from an EU grant meant for improving the entrance road of Tirana. I chose the colors in a not very democratic way. Can it be democratic? I don't think so, because if it's democratic, it's grey. Someone would like orange; someone else would like blue. The compromise between colors is gray.

While the first building is being painted, the owner of the company phones. He says: "Mr. Mayor, something terrible is happening. We started to paint with this color you gave us. There is a traffic jam, there are hundreds of people in front of the building, and there is this French supervisor, who is visibly angry because his skin is dark red, and he is screaming."

So I go there first thing, and there is this French guy who is literally hysterical. It was a very bright orange that was being painted, something like 20 square meters of orange on this large surface. There were about 200 people looking, some laughing, some screaming, and some being shocked.

I ask the French guy what is the problem. He says: "What's the problem? What do you mean what's the problem? Look at this. This is terrible. And this is European taxpayers' money. How can it be used to paint buildings orange? This does not conform to European standards." To which I reply: "All right, then at my first press conference I have to say: forget about Communist censorship, apparently the European Union is even worse. They want to decide what color to paint our buildings." He says: "No, we have to find a compromise." I say: "Sir, compromise is gray, and we have enough gray. So, let us go on."

We went on, and color became the biggest topic of discussion in the poorest country in Europe. You had color discussed on the radio, on TV, and in parliament. It seemed like Albania had been transformed into a café in Montmartre at the time of the Impressionists.

A noisy minority was against all this. I made a survey, which remains my preferred survey in 20 years of politics. The survey asked: "Do you like what is happening in your city with the colors? Do you want it to stop or to continue?" Of the people who took the survey, 67 percent said they liked what was happening,

85 percent said they wanted it to continue. So, half of the people who didn't like it still didn't want it to stop. There are times in life when you have to say, I don't like it but I don't want it to stop either.

HUO: This brings us to the beginning of you being Prime Minister, because very early on you expressed a desire for Albania becoming part of the EU. You said it was, as I quoted earlier, about having the possibility to "place Albania in a safe zone from the curse of history." Given the theme of this year's Convoco Forum, it would be good to hear a bit more about this intention and how it evolved over time.

ER: Europe for us is what it has been for those who imagined it in the first place. This must be why sometimes our friends in Europe look at us as though we are naïve or over-excited. For the first time in its history, Europe has seen three generations without war. For us, Europe is precisely this: the chance to remove ourselves from history into a zone where we are safe from war. For us, war is not some black-and-white documentary about Hitler on Netflix. We had war in the Balkans. I was Minister of Culture when we received 500,000 refugees who were being pushed out of Kosovo because of ethnic cleansing. For us in the region, Europe is first and foremost a project of peace and co-operation for the good of the next generations. So, we can't give up on that. Of course, when you see Britain leaving and Albania wanting to enter, something doesn't really match up. It's easier to divorce than to prevent a marriage.

We are in love and when you are in love, whatever your parents, your friends and whoever will say, if you want to be married, you get married, that's it. Although the European Union is not doing well, to say the least, we still want to be a part of it. It's not that we want to join Europe and give more headaches to the big guys who are already fed up with some of the newcomers. We want to build a European country and a European region that are governed by institutions, by the rule of law, and by functioning democracies. There is only one way to do it. It's Europe.

I strongly believe we are a country of Muslims and Christians. We have different kinds of Muslims and different kinds of Christians. I am Catholic. My wife is Muslim. Our two kids from our respective first marriages are Orthodox. Now we have a new one together. I don't know what he will choose to be. Maybe he'll decide to be Jewish, and that'll be fine.

The thing is this: what brings us all together is Europe. What makes our lives easier somehow is

Europe. What makes Europe's life more difficult, however, is that there is no shared story. There was a fascist story, there was a Communist story, and there was a liberal story. Now, there is a collection of different stories, but there is not a common story.

HUO: Of course, there are EU values and there are Albanian values. It would be interesting to hear about that negotiation and also about your personal vision for Europe.

ER: EU values and Albanian values—that's a difficult negotiation. But let me say one thing. Albania was the only country in Europe that had more Jews after the war than before the war. It's the only country in Europe where no Jew was released to the Nazis. Muslim families adopted Jews. The Albanian Catholic Cardinal made a lot of fake baptisms to give Jews a Catholic identity. When the Nazis convoked the religious leaders, who were the only authority in the country after the occupation, the Nazis said: "We want to sign an agreement with you. You have to agree that the gold that was transferred to Rome should be taken by us, and you have to agree that the list of Jews should be handed over." They signed over the gold, but not the Jews.

I think it's a big value that in our little, poor country, opening the doors and sheltering people is not something you would put in question. You just do it. I think it's a European value, no?

We have a strange past, and our first constitution, our canon, states in the first clause that the house of the Albanians belongs to God and to the guests. Hospitality is a religion in Albania. It was and it still is.

Our country passed through many hardships during the democratic transition. We had pyramid schemes collapse, leading to unrest with 4,000 people dead in 1997—it was nearly a civil war—but we never had a foreigner touched.

A British journalist came to Albania in the middle of this blow-up. Everyone was armed. People lost all their savings in these pyramid schemes. Of course, it was dangerous. He wrote an article that said: "If you're a foreigner, you can visit Albania because it's dangerous for Albanians, but not for anyone else. Don't listen to people that say you can get killed, you can get raped, or you can get robbed. Yes, of course, be careful. If you stay at the Rogner Hotel, the Austrian hotel in Tirana, they might rip you off with the telephone bill." Austrians stealing—this was the only thing that could happen to you in Albania as a foreigner at that time. It was a Brit who said this.

Albania is in the Western Balkans surrounded by EU borders. I'm sure that 99 percent of parliamentarians in the EU parliament don't even know this. When they hear about the Western Balkans and Albania and other people wanting to join, they probably think these guys are where Turkey ends, or somewhere beyond Ukraine. No, we are inside.

During the refugee crisis, refugees would enter the EU through Greece, would exit in North Macedonia and Serbia, and would re-enter through Croatia or Hungary. What's the point of leaving out this space where people are very much believing in the idea of being part of this big family?

What is the difference between a young Muslim in our region and a young Muslim in, let's say, Iraq? The difference is that our young Muslim has the dream of Europe, the prospect of a way of living and of contributing to the world that is paved by values and by tradition. For the young Muslim in Iraq, where is the perspective?

So it's very important to understand that, yes, we are Europeans, and being part of the Union for us is a matter of belonging once and forever to a space of values and people that is the best in the world.

HUO: We have all seen images over the last couple of weeks in relation to the local elections of June 30. These images are quite disruptive of what we think of the new Albania. Can you tell us about that?

ER: Yes, maybe I can. I don't know. I'm biased. If you invited the other side, you would hear a completely different story. That is the beauty of living in a democracy. You have totally different stories sometimes. One thing Communism did among many other things, which has defined our life even after Communism faded away, is eliminating for everyone the idea of the Other. There was no Other. There were only enemies. So, it was us and the enemies. The idea of the opponent was never part of our mindset.

You can overthrow a regime in three days when the time has come, but I don't know if one generation or two are enough to change the mindset. Communism is somehow like Chernobyl. You have the blow, you have the people that are killed, you have the people that are wounded, but then you also have the legacy of malformations.

Detoxing our mindset is not easy. Why am I saying this in trying to answer your question? Because we have a very tough political life. I strongly believe that the quality of democracy, the quality of living together, does not depend on how much you agree, but on the ways in which you disagree. Our quality of life in politics is frankly very low. Democracy is not an easy exercise, and growing up and maturing is part of this painful period of transition.

European integration is unique because of this. It gives you the tools to modernize. It gives you the know-how to build institutions and a credible justice system. Combining the know-how of Europe with the attraction Europe has on Albanians, you can make reforms that are very unpopular but that still have big support. Because people say to themselves, okay, this is not nice, but we have to do it because we are Europeans, and we want to belong to Europe.

This Europe of many speeds, I think it's part of the discussion within the European Union. They need to reform, because this organization with 28 members, well, 27 now, or maybe there'll be 28 again, it doesn't work. It's a lot of vested interests, a lot of bureaucracy. It needs to be reformed.

I can understand well the French President when he says it doesn't work with 27 members, let alone with six more states coming from the craziest part of Europe, the Western Balkans. But at the same time, I don't get it when people in Europe do not understand the importance of the integration process for us.

The journey is much more important than the arrival, because through the journey, we can modernize, we can create the states we never had in our history, and we can possess the know-how that Europe has.

HUO: This is your journey in politics and, as we initially said, there is your journey in art. Of course, your journey in art never stops, you do many exhibitions, and you participated in the Venice Biennale. Two years ago, you had an exhibition in Berlin. It's always your drawings that continue. You do these doodles in meetings, and you do them in your office as well, you do them when you travel. They sometimes become wallpaper. More recently, you went from these 2D drawings into 3D drawings. You actually started to make a lot of ceramics. So, there is no end to experimentation in your visual art, and it would be great, because we started with art, to talk a bit about these more recent works.

ER: When I became Minister of Culture, after the burial of my father, I thought I had buried the artist in myself. But it all started again out of boredom, out of the impossibility of tolerating government meetings. For me, being a member of the government was a totally new life. Never before did I have to deal with paperwork. Having hours of discussions on topics from the police to the environment, I was always drawing. We had weekly sessions, and after every session, the Minister of Education, who sat on my right-hand side, would ask: "Can I take it?"

One day I go to his office, and he says: "I want to show you my art collection." He had put all my art in this nice file. I thought, oh my God, this is art. The guy seemed to me like a thief. But I couldn't say anything, so I went back to my office terrified and told my assistant this guy was a thief. She smiled and said: "Don't worry, you have hundreds of them."

She opened her cupboard, and apparently, I was drawing all the time in my office too, and she was collecting. Before I became Mayor, the drawings had been black-and-white. When I became Mayor, I had colors on my table to indicate the colors of the buildings. Then the drawings started to become like that, too.

All the time, during the meetings, the phone calls, and my moments of solitude, I draw. Only when I meet foreigners I don't do it, because they will not understand. Once I had a friend come to me for some reason. He said: "Listen, I know that with power comes arrogance, but it's better to tell me to get out than to be so selfish to do your drawing while I am telling you that I have a big problem." I said it was not meant that way and stopped. Then, after a while of him talking, he asked me whether I was following. I said: "No, I'm not following, let me draw. If I draw I follow, otherwise I'm not here." He replied, "Okay, please draw." My suggestion is to draw during meetings because you'll retain much more information from the meeting, and you will be far less stressed when you react.

HUO: This connects of course to the conversation I had with Umberto Eco in which he talked about the importance of having artists in the EU. He was also telling me that we needed to do something about the disappearance of doodling and handwriting, because in the digital age, less and less people do that. So, it's also a form of protest. I devote my entire Instagram to that every day to keep doodling alive.

Now, recently you went into 3D. You're doing amazing ceramics. But besides that, you also put art in the Center for Openness and Dialogue in Tirana. It's a whole organization for which you commission artists like Carsten Höller, Thomas Demand, Flaka Haliti, and Philippe Parreno to do projects. It would be interesting to hear a bit about the Center for Openness and, as we wrap up the conversation, I would be particularly interested to hear about Carsten Höller's *Triple Giant Mushroom*.

ER: I had never sculpted before. It was a friend of mine, a sculptor, who took my drawings and made some plates and teacups for my mother with my drawings without asking my permission.

I did not like it. But I liked the gesture. So, I thought I would go to him, thank him for doing it, but ask him not to do it anymore. I went, and his ceramic studio was full of these vases made with fresh clay. I touched the clay, and I got it. I started to go every Sunday. It became my gym. Instead of running, I went to deal with the clay. It was fantastic because it was the only hours in my life without a mobile phone, the perfect digital detox.

The Centre for Openness and Dialogue is something else. Before becoming Prime Minister, I always said if one day I become Prime Minister, the office building would not have fences anymore. The Prime Minister's office and residence looked like a prison with fences and soldiers. I always believed that buildings protect themselves through beauty, not through fences. A beautiful building is more intimidating than an ugly building with fences.

So I took off the fences and the whole first floor was opened up to the public and became a Centre for Openness and Dialogue. We have exhibitions, we have a public library, we have a little movie theater where kids can come and project their movies. We also have discussions there.

I said that protestors could come and use the Centre for free, and if they wanted, I could come, and other Ministers could join also and discuss with them. But protestors have a problem with discussion because if they discuss, then they are not protestors anymore. So, it's not easy, but still it's also there for this.

We had some very generous contributions from Thomas Demand, who practically was the artist that opened the Center. We had a beautiful show of his work. We had a Philippe Parreno donation, the beautiful *Marquee, Tirana* light sculpture in the entrance of the building, which was very controversial. It still is. My opponent friends want to break it. But until now, it has survived.

But Carsten Höller's *Triple Giant Mushroom* sculpture, which was put in the garden, didn't survive the assault of the protestors. They broke it, and of course it was a sad moment. It was also difficult to explain to Carsten that it was not an aesthetic protest, but a political one. It was against me, not against the sculpture. They couldn't get me, so they broke the mushroom.

I was very happy when Carsten called me after a month and said he had a great idea. He said we'd do it again, but we'd do it 25 percent higher. Whoever will touch it will know that it will only come back taller. This will prevent people from harming the mushroom. I find this idea beautiful. It's like surviving by growing and reacting by coming back. Life goes on.

HUO: My last question, Edi, the question I always ask in every conversation is about unrealized projects. We know a lot about architects' unrealized projects because they publish them quite regularly, and it's actually very productive. By publishing them, they often get them built. But we know almost nothing about artists', poets', writers', and, as a matter of fact, also politicians' unrealized projects.

There are many categories of the unbuilt. There are projects that are too big to be realized. There are also projects that are too small to be realized. There are projects that are censored, and then, as Doris Lessing once told me, there are projects that are self-censored. I think we all have projects that we have not yet dared to do. So, in this whole complex of the unrealized, I want to ask you to tell us about one unrealized project you would like to do.

ER: The painted buildings, which were meant just to cheer up the community, showed how powerful beauty could be against crime, social disruption, marginalization, and weakness in the relationship between citizens and institution. In painted roads, we achieved 100 percent municipal tax collection, which, when I started as a Mayor, was down to 4 percent. People would not pay municipal tax, as they would not even consider that the municipality existed because the city was in such a disastrous state. We also saw a significant lowering of crime in general.

One day I was crossing one of these painted roads while we were doing some final works, and I saw a family replacing the fences around their shop with beautiful glass. The man said: "Now it's safe." I asked why. He replied: "The government has brought more police." I asked, "What police?" He said: "It's beautiful. Look, there are lights, there are colors, the pavement is nice, and there are trees." It was instinctive, this feeling of safety.

Then I started to invite artists to paint buildings. This was the second phase. It attracted lots of tourists. I asked the artists just to send pictures. They would make the model, and then we would realize it. Lots of artists, like Olafur Eliasson, came to paint buildings, all for free.

Then, in the third phase, I wanted to team up with a big paint company, saying: "Listen, give us the amount of paint to transform the city into an urban art museum by giving different artists different neighborhoods so that we have one normal map with addresses and another one with the names of artists." The idea was that you would go to the Gerhard Richter neighborhood or to the Olafur Eliasson Park. This project needed a very serious amount of paint. The company involved would have fantastic publicity. It could make a catalogue, showing people how it can change their lives. But I didn't find this visionary company. So, this is an unrealized project.

HUO: It could not be a more wonderful conclusion. Edi, thank you so much.

CHAPTER 12

RETHINK MARKETS: CRITERIA FOR AN AGILE COMPETITION POLICY

MATTHIAS KARL

The digital economy presents major challenges not only to industry, manufacturing, and services, but also to administration, government, and the entire education sector. In the face of such fundamental revolutions, it is inevitable that the law will also be affected by digital changes, in particular in two ways. On the one hand, the law must deal with digital transformation as a regulatory phenomenon, i.e. as a real-life context, and on the other, the law itself must become digital and cannot disregard digitalization when it comes to its own manifestations, applications, and procedures.

Of course, not all legal fields are affected to the same extent, and progress in the implementation process varies from field to field. While in Germany civil law already has comprehensive rules covering e-commerce, classic regulatory patterns persist in other legal fields, and land sales still require notarial instruments that include the reading aloud of contracts that are now often "smart contracts" created by artificial intelligence. Nevertheless, radical change, whether slow or fast, can be seen everywhere, and one day even inheritance law will include regulations covering how a will written onto a blockchain can deal with the possible exclusion of heirs. In this respect, it is unsurprising that competition and antitrust law too cannot escape this transformation, and several commissions, expert reports, and draft legislation are already specifically examining the issue of how to address the phenomena of the digital world in terms of competition policy.

For competition and antitrust law, however, this sometimes disruptive transformation creates a particular dilemma. After all, this disruptive transformation precisely describes Schumpeter's notion of "creative destruction", making it the original form of competition.[1] Should competition policy stand by in astonishment, and simply let this kind of competition happen, precisely because it is new and a textbook example of the "process of discovery" (to quote Schumpeter again) or the "most ingenious instrument of disempowerment," as Franz Böhm described it?[2] Or is there not a need to modify the rules of competition, to intervene and shape them actively, because the competitive playing field is breaking down established and accepted parameters? Does this intervention have to be long-term and made at arm's length, or can it also happen quickly, selectively, and therefore in an agile way?

In this essay, I would like to highlight the option of an agile competition policy, but in so doing not lose sight of the extent to which agility within a regulatory framework is at all possible, without denying the law its qualities as a controlling, safeguarding, and regulating entity. This raises the question of how competition policy must be oriented over the long term, what degree of tenacity it can show, and how controlling or even interventionist it may be.

This question is not merely academic; in practice it is highly topical. After nearly a decade of consensus, German and European antitrust and merger control law is being dragged into the limelight of political debate. The argument displays a fierceness that shows alarmingly how political discourse makes use of populist clichés even when addressing complex issues. For example, anyone who demands drastic reforms in competition policy immediately arouses the general suspicion that they want to eliminate competition as a neo-liberalist principle and favor protectionism. The other camp, meanwhile, fears that Europe with its system of free and unfettered competition will be torn between Asia's strategic state-controlled economies and the interventionist trade policy of the United States.

My thesis is that competition policy can be agile, that it must exist within a normative framework, and that its measures and criteria must be modified in such a way that it can get to grips with even fast-moving transformation processes.

In support of my first thesis, I want to show that competition policy was actually more dynamic in recent years than is remembered today, and therefore that reforming and modifying the regulatory framework may seem completely justified and not an unduly zealous intervention into cast-iron principles.

For example, it is unquestionable that the key objectives of the European Treaties include the implementation of the European fundamental freedoms and the protection of free and undistorted competition. The completion of the European Single Market should be clearly pursued in free-market terms. Although the European Treaties[3] state as their objective that the

Union and the Member States must ensure that the conditions necessary for industrial competitiveness within the Union are guaranteed, nevertheless the Union's actions to that end must be carried out within a system of open and competitive markets.

This leads to a clear substantive limitation of industrial policy competencies in favor of a market-based competition policy and a ban on dirigiste and interventionist industrial policy. This objective is also served by the central provisions of European and equivalent German antitrust law, that is the prohibition of anti-competitive agreements and concerted practices, a prohibition of the abuse of a dominant market position, and merger control rules that aim at preventing the creation of consortia if the latter compromise effective competition.

Although these principles should apply to all sectors of the economy, the Treaty on the Functioning of the European Union allows for substantial exceptions, in particular in the cases of agriculture and the transport sector. Up until July 22, 2002, there was a special antitrust law for coal and steel, as this economic sector was considered so important that it should not be exposed to the system of free competition. From this we can deduce first of all that sector-specific exceptions to the fundamental principle of the free-market system and undistorted competition are well known and have been approved for years. Likewise, an ongoing evolution of the current antitrust law can also be seen operating through legislative measures such as the adoption of European regulations and directives and the case law of the Luxembourg courts.

Block exemption regulations in particular have created a large number of very detailed provisions that deal in some cases with highly delicate regulatory details, for example in questions of distribution policy in the case of geo-blocking or the discount policy for online retailers or bricks-and-mortar retail stores.

Here it must be recognized that modifications to Europe's legal framework take place through extremely long-term processes. However, this is not due to respect for the subject matter of antitrust alone, but also to the inherently long drawn-out nature of the European legislative process. However, from this we should not derive a principle that a faster and more agile modification of competition regulations would immediately be afflicted with the odium of interventionism. The example of the introduction of European merger control can show that there was not always clear agreement within the European Community on the need for this instrument in pursuing the objective of a market economic system, but that for a long time there was a lot of controversy about the right objectives.

As early as the 1955 Messina Conference it was certainly discussed that the Community's policy objective should be to draw up rules allowing the control of mergers wherever they lead to dominant market positions and thereby jeopardize the establishment of the Common Market. This demand, laid down in the so-called *Spaak Report*, was followed in 1965 by a European Commission memorandum on the problem of the concentration of businesses in the Common Market. However, it was not mentioned again until the final declaration of the October 1972 Paris summit, which aimed to ensure that business mergers within the Community take place only in accordance with the economic and social objectives of the Community. A first proposal for a merger regulation in July 1973 was followed by amendments in 1981, 1984, and 1986. It was only the European Court of Justice's Philip Morris decision in 1987,[4] judging a competitor's acquisition of stock to be a relevant issue in the prohibition of cartels, which led to the enactment of the European Merger Regulation on September 21, 1990.[5] This instrument was modified slightly in 2004, when the substantive assessment criterion of a merger—the creation or strengthening of a dominant position—was complemented by the additional requirement that it present a significant impediment to effective competition.

The history of European merger control thus shows that its existence and application is not a mandatory component of the market economy, but rather a dynamic instrument for achieving the Single Market objective of undistorted effective competition. The authors of the 1956 *Spaak Report* regarded the main problem concerning the concentration of businesses as the fact that the desired opening up of markets between Member States would once again be jeopardized by mergers when tariffs and quotas were abolished. This concern was superseded by fears that, without merger controls, there would be an unfettered surge of American and Japanese companies into the Common Market. Today this concern has been superseded by a "theory of harm," which has latterly focused on consumer benefits within the Single Market.

I conclude from this that the demand for an agile competition policy is fundamentally consistent with the evolution of European law so far, and that the modification of competition regulations to chime with global economic activity does not contradict or jeopardize the objectives of the Community and the market economy, but is ultimately committed to its consistent evolution.

This brings me to the question of the criteria needed for assessing effective competition and the standards to be applied. Here again the problem arises that state intervention, i.e. the activities of antitrust authorities, intrudes into competition, while the aim of such protection is free competition itself, and state intrusion into the competition process is regarded negatively as an intervention. So what would be seen as good and legitimate state intervention into competition, the kind of intervention that guarantees a system of undistorted competition and does not influence, create, or perpetuate competitive structures in a dirigiste way? In both the European Union and all market-oriented legal systems, the decisive criterion for legitimate antitrust state intervention is that it prevents the abuse of a dominant market position and, in the field of merger control, that it prevents the creation or strengthening of a dominant market position.

Market dominance is thus the central issue in evaluating the benchmark for legitimate intervention into competition policy. According to the European Court of Justice's definition, a dominant market position exists when a company by virtue of its economic position is able to hinder the maintenance of effective competition in the relevant market, allowing it to behave to an appreciable extent independently of its competitors, customers, and ultimately consumers.

The starting point for this central question is therefore the definition of the relevant market where the company's dominant position exists. Thus, while case law and legislation have repeatedly dealt with the criteria of market dominance, the determination of the market, i.e. market definition, is often beyond the reach of normative standards.

On the issue of market dominance, German law states that it relates to the relevant product and geographic market.[6] A legal, that is normative stipulation of how the relevant product and geographic market must be defined is not specified by the Act. Equally, the question of market definition is not addressed in the guidelines on market dominance issued by the German Federal Cartel Office's merger control. A preliminary legal determination of market definition can be found in Germany's Act against Restraints of Competition (GWB), which states that the assumption of a market shall not be invalidated by the fact that a good or service is provided free of charge.[7]

German legislation has thus made it clear that it is responding to the economic realities of the digital economy and has made the concept of the market independent of whether or not revenue is generated. However, the criteria for determining product and geographic relevance remain undecided both in the GWB and in European law. This brings us to the crucial question of whether market definition is a purely empirical process or a concept that must be created on a normative basis. Debates arise continually on this subject, and opinions are admittedly divided. While the German Federal Cartel Office likes to say that market definition is the best-kept secret of the antitrust authorities, companies are making ever louder demands for an accurate market definition, one with at least normatively underpinned standards and evaluation criteria. In this respect, the debate about the Siemens/Alstom decision and the failed Thyssen/Tata merger makes no sense[8] if it is assumed that critics of the decision to block the mergers wanted to create European champions at the expense of European consumers—champions whose persistent structural conservativism rendered them anti-innovation. This debate can be immediately defused of its emotion if we focus on the initial question of "how can the relevant product and geographic market be defined?" Which temporal dimensions should be applied to market activity? Which evaluation period should be used? What requirements must be met to prove the existence of a global market? What extent of proof is needed when assessing future developments?

So far, European and German legislation have both shied away from this and shifted verification to the courts, which must then retrospectively develop normative standards to apply to the antitrust authorities' empirical evidence.

As a way of stimulating debate I would like to present the thesis that legislation must deal more intensively with the question of which normative requirements must exist in order to produce an appropriate definition of the market. Admittedly, this is difficult because it requires a description of a dynamic business activity which cannot easily be translated into legal language. On the other hand, competition policy cannot rely on the courts being able to freely develop the appropriate standards, in order to determine the factual accuracy of a market definition and the ensuing question of market dominance. To return to the example of Siemens/Alstom: assuming a global market, the market share of Siemens and Alstom was said to be low and blocking the deal would not have been possible.[9] By rejecting the global market and assuming a European market, Siemens/Alstom currently enjoys a high market share. What are the benchmarks by which European jurisdiction should judge which is the correct market definition? A truly legitimate competition policy can no longer ignore the question of how, in a system of undistorted competition, one should define relevant product and geographic markets. This is not an easy task, but the instruments to do it have already been described many times in the current debate. It is time for policy-makers to bring the already-existing, relevant, normative provisions into the legislative process and enshrine them correspondingly in current antitrust rules.

Alongside this, short-term changes in antitrust law may also be appropriate. This has already been provided for in German legislation[10] and programmatically laid down. Thus, an obligation to evaluate is enshrined in the law that obliges the Federal Ministry for Economic Affairs and Energy to make legislative bodies report on their experiences with the regulations three years after the entry into force of the additions and specifications introduced with respect to the digital economy.[11] This can only mean that legislation operates subsequently on the basis of these experiences and either confirms the functionality and accuracy of the chosen specifications or makes the appropriate modifications. Agile competition policy thus presupposes normative specifications and, at the same time, accepts that these specifications must be constantly reviewed and, if necessary, modified. In this respect, I consider my thesis of the normative anchoring of market definition criteria in law to be acceptable too, since dynamic economic development requires specifications on the one hand, but on the other hand must also allow for the possibility of modifications, without being labeled as interventionist.

Perhaps this will even lead to the development of entirely new criteria beyond a market-related perspective, and an open concept will emerge which I will call "competition dominance" and which supersedes the concept of market dominance. I see this as an opportunity to account for future phenomena in terms of cartel law, phenomena that can arise in the digital economy without a direct relationship to the market. For example, we might imagine competition for the "attention time" of the person who is in a driverless car and not concentrating, or competition for access to media in blockchain-based decentralized storage networks. Of course, somewhere behind all these concepts lie the market processes of exchange, but competition is already taking place in the upstream pathways, in the platforms, data managers, influencers, search engines, or gatekeepers. They define pre-market competition that would be worth protecting even before the establishment of a dominant market position.

Finally, I would like to comment briefly on the procedural component of an agile competition policy, as it is frequently argued that taking on board the theses I have put forward might lead to a near-inflationary accumulation of antitrust amendments, all of which would lead to further bureaucracy, reporting obligations, and bureaucratic burdens. And ultimately, it is argued, an interventionist competition policy would arise again, which cannot lead to sensible results due to a lack of resources.

Here I would counter that agile competition policy can be made possible by a reorientation of the antitrust authorities, and that no new regulators are needed to oversee the digital world. Looking at the workload of the European Commission / Directorate-General for Competition or the German Federal Cartel Office from the point of view of practitioners, it is striking how to a very considerable extent work is undertaken that is completely irrelevant to competition, tying up resources which are then not available when it comes to applying the necessary legal enforcement. Almost all antitrust authorities complain about staff shortages, but ineffective work processes and decision-making structures exist in many antitrust proceedings. For example, in approximately 1,200 merger control proceedings per year, the German Federal Cartel Office resolves over 90 percent without remedies. The fact that such a high number of cases resolved without remedies are reported is due to flaws in the registration threshold. The jurisdiction of the Cartel Office is already invoked if all the companies concerned generate total global turnover of €500 million, with for example one of the companies concerned having domestic sales of €25 million and the other €5 million. Transactions undertaken by every larger medium-sized enterprise are thus subject to merger control. While uncomplicated cases are dealt with quickly and concluded, however, even if they are processed quickly, 1,000 cases still mean 1,000 procedures for which a file has to be created, checks carried out, costs charged, and a notice of clearance issued.

By comparison, Swiss merger control, for example, requires companies to register a transaction in Switzerland if each of the concerned companies generates CHF 100 million or more in turnover in Switzerland. Unsurprisingly, the workload of the Swiss Competition Commission is much smaller in terms of merger control, and yet Swiss policy does not consider the market economy and a system of undistorted competition to be under threat in Switzerland. Comparing the significance of mergers, an increase in the merger control registration threshold to €100 million in domestic revenue in each case would certainly be justified for the German economy. Companies with lower domestic turnover are not a threat to the existence of the market economy and cannot in principle restrict freedom of competition. A streamlining of antitrust law is long overdue both at German and at European level.

Equally, this argument cannot be disputed by the fact that in certain niche markets, where only small- and medium-sized enterprises are operating, this can result in high market shares and concomitant disadvantages for the consumer. At national and European level, we need a *de minimis* market limit, which exempts from merger control markets with a Europe-wide volume of €100 million, and where there are no end consumers on the opposite side of the market. Markets in transition to global status or who are on the way to replacing mature, perhaps dying, technologies must not be held back by prohibition decisions that prevent necessary structural adjustments. Again, this is not about creating national champions, but an agile reaction to upheaval in technology markets that does not directly disadvantage the end users.

Through the measures outlined above, antitrust authorities can free up the resources needed to monitor digital competition, develop appropriate criteria, and transform the legislative process.

"Rethink markets" would thus be the slogan of my program for an agile competition policy, a program that

1. means a new kind of evaluation without departing from the principle of free competition, but developing it;

2. demands a necessary, normative specification of the intervention standards; and

3. means consistently re-focusing and de-cluttering the antitrust authorities' obsolete approaches to auditing.

This will enable the creation of a framework in which Europe can face up to digital challenges and successfully assimilate into a system of free and undistorted competition.

Notes

1. Joseph Schumpeter's (1883–1950) concept of "creative destruction" describes a continual process of innovation, driven by competition, which "incessantly revolutionizes the economic structure *from within*, incessantly destroying the old one, incessantly creating a new one." And this process of "creative destruction" is the "essential fact about capitalism." Joseph A. Schumpeter, *Capitalism, Socialism, and Democracy*, 3rd edn. (New York: Harper and Brothers, 1950), p. 83.

2. Franz Böhm (1895–1977) described competition as "the most ingenious instrument of disempowerment" as it protects consumers from exploitation by private businesses and thus

promotes social equality. See Franz Böhm, "Die Bedrohung der Freiheit durch private ökonomische Macht in der heutigen Gesellschaft" in *Universitas* 18 (1963), pp. 37–48.

3. As amended by Article 173 of the Treaty on the Functioning of the European Union.

4. British-American Tobacco Company Ltd and R. J. Reynolds Industries Inc. v Commission of the European Communities, *European Court Reports 1987 -04487*, ECLI:EU:C:1987:490.

5. This was preceded by the re-drafting of the merger regulation and then the original version of Regulation 4064/89 on December 21, 1989.

6. See Section 18 of the Act against Restraints of Competition (GWB).

7. See Section 18 (2) (a) of the Act against Restraints of Competition (GWB).

8. The planned merger of Siemens Mobility and Alstom was blocked by the EU Commission on February 6, 2019; the planned merger of Thyssenkrupp and Tata Steel was blocked on June 11, 2019. On Siemens/Alstom, see: https://ec.europa.eu/commission/presscorner/detail/en/IP_19_881 (accessed December 17, 2019); on Thyssenkrupp/Tata, see: https://ec.europa.eu/commission/presscorner/detail/en/STATEMENT_19_2954 (accessed December 17, 2019).

9. See Note 8.

10. See the 9th Amendment to the Act against Restraints of Competition (GWB).

11. See Section 18 (8) and Section 43 (a) of the Act against Restraints of Competition (GWB).

CHAPTER 13

FREEDOM IS NOT THE ABSENCE OF REGULATION

IN CONVERSATION WITH RUPPRECHT PODSZUN

Convoco talked to Rupprecht Podszun about European competition policy in today's digital world.

Convoco: Competition policy has always been a defining pillar of the European project. The idea of competition law is to have open markets and to make companies compete on merit to the benefit of the consumer. You say that competition policy is at a crossroads today. Why is that?

Rupprecht Podszun: We have to make choices about how to shape the digital economy: is it an economy organized by monopolistic gatekeepers or is it run according to the mechanism of competition? The rules and tools to protect competition were designed at a time when the European economy was driven by coal and steel, and when economic policy was very much guided by normative beliefs. You may remember the "Ordoliberals," a generation of economic policy analysts in the 1950s who developed a framework for doing business that was guaranteed by the state or the European institutions.

This framework is still there but the digital economy plays a different style of hardball. There are phenomena such as big data, network effects, platforms, digital ecosystems—just to mention a few buzzwords. Some of our rules and tools simply do not fit very well with these phenomena. There has also been a change of attitude in conceptualization: we lack a widely shared idea of how to secure the fundamental freedoms in markets. Economic theory has become much more sophisticated since the times of the Ordoliberals—and more empirical, too. That makes it difficult to define what we want from an economic perspective and from a political one.

C: Margrethe Vestager has been reappointed as the European Commissioner in charge of competition and she has a remarkable track record of hefty fines against Google and clawing back taxes from Apple.

RP: Her determination is indeed outstanding, yet the decisions still have to pass the legal test in the European courts. The fines are one thing, the "remedies" are more important: will there be a significant change of behavior that opens up markets? Some of the proceedings came late or took a long time—the first Google case, Google Shopping, took seven years of investigations. That is an eternity in such markets. We have also seen failures in competition enforcement. For instance, Facebook was allowed to buy WhatsApp and Instagram. We are not yet able to control "killer acquisitions" where the GAFAs—Google, Amazon, Facebook, Apple—buy small potential rivals as soon as they show up on stage. So, yes, Commissioner Vestager is inspiring, but there is a long way to go.

C: Do you think European competition law is up to the task?

RP: The next two years are decisive; there is a reform agenda on the table. Germany will make a start in

2020 with new legislation and the European Union will follow suit. We need to come up with a regulatory framework for the digital economy. We need to be brave! We need to focus on innovation! And we need not fall prey to lobbyists for outdated business models on the one hand or for the tech giants on the other! This is not just an issue for competition law, though. Access to data probably needs sectoral regulation—holding platforms accountable needs new regulation. And, obviously, Europe needs to invest in research, the digital single market, and a better infrastructure. Not to create a new Google, but to enable entrepreneurs and scientists to take the next big steps.

C: Regulation is not really a popular word with start-ups.

RP: It is a misperception to see the absence of formal regulation as freedom. If there is no framework, rules are set by the strongest actors. This is what we witness today in large parts of the Internet. Take Google as an example. It is the gatekeeper of searches and the operator of Android. For many aspects of our economic decisions, Google has defined the boundaries—or taken the decision for us. Users and companies are increasingly locked in. That is not freedom. Still, the reservations towards regulation have their merits. When I talk about regulation, I mean smart and adaptive regulation. We need to get away from setting principles in stone that are out of touch the day the lengthy legislative process is over.

C: The Bundeskartellamt tried to go after Facebook for privacy violations, yet the order was stopped by the Düsseldorf Higher Regional Court in interim proceedings. You interpreted this as a clash of two institutions.

RP: On the one hand, there is the Bundeskartellamt, where teams of lawyers and economists work together for years on a case. Thought leaders there are heavily involved in international policy debates. The agency is also in a sort of competition to come up with pioneering solutions to the problems of highly concentrated digital markets. On the other hand, you have a bench of three honorable judges, sharp-minded lawyers, completely independent. Their worries are not so much directed at the question of "how to tame the tech titans," rather they very soberly examine whether the approach is in accordance with the rules, with traditional doctrine, with precedent. Both institutions do perfectly what they should do, yet in new and innovative cases these different institutional starting points may clash.

C: There are reports that the US agencies are also taking a closer look what the GAFA companies are doing.

RP: Indeed. US antitrust was a pretty dull experience in the last decade: nothing to see. Enforcement was weak, and concentration is on the rise in the US in a worrying way. One reason seems to be that enforcement in antitrust law is more politicized. The Antitrust Division of the Department of Justice does not enjoy the same independence as its European counterparts. Equally, laissez-faire economics, the "Chicago School," still resonates with competition law judges in the United States. It is good to see international consensus is now growing.

C: You have not yet spoken about the calls for more industrial policy and European champions that came up after the prohibition of the Siemens/Alstom merger.

RP: True, the German and the French ministers of economics were furious that the European Commission stopped that merger. They pointed at competition from state-funded enterprises from China. We often had such calls for European champions before. I do not worry too much; I am confident they will return to sound economic liberalism. The debate even had three positive aspects:

first, the debate about China and how to establish a level playing field was helpful. Second, the debate triggered proposals for economic policies that may turn out to be fruitful. And third, the outrageous proposal to create an instrument to overrule the European Commission in merger cases energized the competition community. We know much better now what we love about tough competition enforcement!

C: That sounds quite confident, overall.

RP: Call me a dreamer, but I believe in the power of reason and in the virtues of the law. Competition law is about taming the powerful. This is the core value that it stands for in the modern European order: economic powerhouses, even monopolies, are subject to a rule-based control by democratic, legitimate institutions. What a fascinating piece of civilization! Globally, competition agencies have flourished.

Just think of the Facebook case, and we can begin to appreciate the beauty and the power of this mechanism. A small agency in Bonn, Germany, scrutinizes the behavior of a company that is worth three-digit-billion dollars. And now they meet in court where three independent judges hear the case and try to find out whether that giant company and that agency adhered to the rules that were agreed on. Once their decision is out, a senate of another court will review it. And we are able to discuss all that and to contribute our ideas and views. Welcome to a competition for the best ideas on how to deal with big business in the future—that's exciting, it's gripping, and it's to the benefit of society. That is exactly the reason why we want competition.

CHAPTER 14

HOW SHOULD GERMANY AND EUROPE DEAL WITH THE GROWING IMPORTANCE OF CHINA?

JÖRG ROCHOLL

INTRODUCTION

Economic relations between Europe and China are gaining more and more interest and are now of fundamental importance for both parties. In Europe, this is particularly true for Germany, because China is Germany's most important trading partner, in some areas well ahead of traditional trading partners such as France, the Netherlands, or the United States. In 2018

Germany exported goods to the value of €93.1 billion to China, which means that German exports to China have almost tripled over the last ten years. During the same period, imports from China actually reached €106.2 billion. There is thus a high degree of interdependency in the exchange of goods and services.

China's increasing importance is primarily due to the ongoing dynamic growth of its economy. Even though Chinese economic growth has long ceased to be in double digits and despite question marks over the official statistics provided by the government in Beijing, with growth of 6.6 percent in 2018, China remains a global engine of growth. By comparison, global economic output increased by only 3.2 percent last year.

If we look at the highest-valued listed companies in the world, we can see evidence that is alarming for Europe and auspicious for China. According to a current EY ranking, American and Chinese companies in particular are among the world's leading companies in this core dimension, while European and especially German companies are increasingly falling behind. Of the latter, only two are in the top 100, with SAP in 51st place and Siemens in 100th place; by contrast, before the financial crisis in 2007, the top 100 still included seven German companies.[1] Two objections can be made here. On the one hand, stock exchange prices are constantly fluctuating so that the picture may look different again tomorrow from what it does today. On the other hand, the German economy in particular benefits from its strong medium-sized companies and the many "hidden champions," which are usually not listed on the stock exchange and thus are not featured in this comparison. In terms of this study, therefore, stock market prices are not the measure of all things, but the trend is clear: capital markets currently consider that the future lies with American and Chinese companies and less with European companies.

Equally, the growing importance of China is not invalidated by the fact that the situation regarding company takeovers and investments has changed in recent times. Chinese investments in Europe have declined significantly over the past year. In the first half of 2019, according to an EY report, they comprised only around $2.4 billion (about €2.2 billion), a decrease of 84 percent compared to the first half of 2018.[2] Investments in Germany were particularly severely affected by this development. While the Chinese invested around $10.1 billion (€9.1 billion) in German companies in the first six months of 2018 (25 transactions), in the first half of 2019 it was just $505 million (11 transactions; €450 million).[3] One could even argue that this decline is linked to the strength of China. As Chinese companies are perceived as more of a competitor in Europe, more thought is given in Europe on how to restrict Chinese companies' access to the domestic market.

CHALLENGES

In dealing with China, there are a number of challenges that do not play a significant role for Germany and German companies when they are trading within the European Union and with other western industrialized countries. Let us now examine some of these challenges more closely.

First, the lack of transparency concerning China's economic development has been repeatedly criticized. This criticism applies not only to the question of the level of actual economic growth, but especially to the borrowing by government and private institutions, and thus to the vulnerability of the Chinese economic model to setbacks and crises. A report by the S&P rating agency in fall 2018 shows that borrowing by Chinese local government institutions beyond their regular accounts has reached $6 trillion, which poses significant risks to financial stability.[4]

Second, when talking about China, the question is often asked whether and to what extent political influence lies behind the economic transactions. The Chinese government has ambitious strategic plans for economic development up to 2025 and 2049. Presumably any lack of knowledge and skills are to be bought in from abroad. This raises the question of the extent to which company acquisitions in other countries serve to transfer and extract technology and know-how. The still relatively small number of cases where Chinese investors have taken over German companies make it difficult to analyze systematically the success of these transactions. However, at least two observations can be derived from the cases that have occurred up till now. On the one hand, the companies that have been taken over and their employees view the cooperation with their Chinese owners as fundamentally positive. This is due, for example, to the generally high level of autonomy that the companies enjoy. At the same time, it has been shown that these acquisitions do not always represent worthwhile investments for the Chinese. A particularly intensively discussed and vivid example of this is Kuka, a German company. The Augsburg manufacturer of industrial robots was often regarded as a showcase company associated with the buzzword "Industry 4.0." As a result, some attempts were made to find new German owners for the company. Ultimately, however, the Chinese refrigerator and air-conditioning manufacturer Midea invested in Kuka in 2015 and took over the company almost completely a year later. With a purchase offer of €115 per share, Midea offered a significant premium of 35 percent above the market value at the time, very effectively preventing other potential investors from making counter bids. This sale ensured a lucrative way out for the original owners. However, the expectations at the time of the takeover have not yet been fulfilled. The production and sale of industrial robots on the one hand and refrigerators on the other have so far produced hardly any synergies, and, as a result, the company's stock market value has decreased significantly since the takeover. We can infer at least two possible interpretations from this. It could be that Midea simply made a bad speculation when acquiring Kuka and could not fulfill its own expectations in terms of growth and synergy. An alternative, more well-intentioned interpretation might be that, for the Chinese, business development alone is not the decisive criterion when it comes to measuring the success of the investment, but another factor is the learning process related to the acquisition of expertise and know-how.

Taking a broader view, people are keeping a critical eye on forums such as the so-called "17 + 1" summit, suspecting that what lies behind this is an attempt by the Chinese to gain influence over international decision-making processes—in this case over Eastern and Central European countries and thus indirectly over the European Union.

Third, there has been criticism of the lack of legal certainty and insufficient protection of intellectual property for foreign investors in China. While critics have seen no noticeable improvement in this area over the past few years, there are also more optimistic opinions, who point out that in China's technological catch-up process the implementation and credible application of patent rights, for example, is in the country's own interest. The latter development is supported by the fact that the process by which China is catching up with and in some areas even overtaking the West technologically is gaining momentum and, at the same time, can be documented better. For instance, the German Federal Government's Expert Commission for Research and Innovation in its annual reports, for example in 2018, has described the promising areas in which China is doing particularly well.

Fourth, the question is asked whether Europe's basic openness towards Chinese investments is mirrored to the same extent by an openness towards international and especially European investments in China. Thus the accusation of a lack of reciprocity in this field continually goes hand-in-hand with the current debates about economic policy, as this is linked to the criticism that China is exploiting the openness of western economic systems, without also granting such openness to companies from other countries. Some prominent examples, such as recent investments by BMW and BASF in China, or developments in majority ownership in the financial industry, show that in this case things are changing. But it is equally clear that there is still a considerable way to go before both parties can achieve the same conditions.

Fifth, there is the fundamental question of the desired future cooperation between companies and the state, in Germany as well. In the case of the Chinese takeover of Kuka, high hopes were initially invested in the possibility that the company might be taken over by other German companies in the role of a so-called "white knight." This possibility quickly evaporated, on the one hand because the price offered by the Chinese buyers was considered by German companies to be too high from a business point of view and was thus a deterrent to a bidding competition. On the other hand, behind closed doors, German companies expressed their concern that an intervention by a German company in the role of a white knight might have negative consequences for this company in China. An intervention, if it were worth attempting at all, could therefore only have taken place at state and not at private level.

WHAT IS TO BE DONE

Europe—especially Germany—and China are economically interdependent. While debates in Germany emphasize first and foremost the country's dependency on China, the high quantities of Chinese exports to Germany, for example, show that this dependency works in both directions. Knowing this brings both opportunities and challenges.

The principle of reciprocity is of central importance in both trade and direct investment. Europe and Germany must continue to push for this principle to be fully and comprehensively implemented—meaning European companies in China should have the same opportunities as Chinese companies have in Europe.

At the same time, Europe needs to further develop its own strengths. The lack of market capitalization among European companies compared to their

American and increasingly also Chinese competitors reveals an urgent need for action, which can be summarized simply—scalability, scalability, scalability! The big question is why American and Chinese platform companies dominate European companies so significantly and outpace them in terms of expected growth rate—despite the enormous success of the European Single Market. At first glance, this market offers all the conditions whereby European companies of all ages and sizes can develop beyond national borders, thus enabling the necessary scalability. The free movement of goods, services, capital, and people is indisputably the central basis for the integration of the European economies and thus for economic growth in Europe. The importance of the Single Market even extends so far that scholars attach greater importance to it in relation to the economic integration of Europe than to the introduction of the single currency in 1999. More than 500 million people live and work in this area, with an economic power that can take on any other economic area worldwide, including China. Thus nobody can seriously dispute the enormous success of the European Single Market and its decisive contribution to economic growth in the European Union over the more than 25 years since its introduction. But can it guarantee this over the next 25 years as well?

It is worth taking a second look here. The economic success of American and Chinese companies with data- and platform-driven business models depends in particular on their fast and extensive scalability, as every new user of a platform increases the value of this platform to all other users. For example, if you want to chat to friends online, you have to go where a lot of friends already are. Beyond a certain critical limit, the number of users grows all the more because nobody can avoid this platform any more. So the magic word is scalability—one might also say growth at any price with a temporary disregard for margins. These follow automatically once you have reached the status of market leader. And then such a platform is not only of interest to users, but also to other actors such as providers of goods and services, capital markets, and financial institutions. So the crucial question is whether the European Single Market can help new business models to achieve scalability. The answer is "yes, but..."

This is because there are still some significant hurdles standing in the way of full market integration in Europe. The key economic and political challenge is to identify these obstacles and remove them as quickly as possible. The concrete economic policy proposal is therefore to create an inventory of all practical hurdles in the European Single Market in order to exploit the untapped potential of full market integration.

Associated with this is the need to further develop Europe's capital markets and thereby promote private investment. The current financial system, particularly in Germany, has proven itself in the past when it comes to financing German companies. To put it simply, the system can be described as follows. Private investors have a great tendency to give their savings to banks in the form of deposits. The banks in turn generate their main income from the interest rate business, i.e. giving loans to private individuals and companies. The latter are financed both in Germany and in other European countries primarily through corporate loans. To enable young companies especially, with their need for venture capital funding, to develop dynamically, this financing model needs to be enhanced at the least, because in Germany in particular there are certainly good opportunities to set up new and innovative companies. By the second or third round of financing at the latest, however, European investors often no longer have sufficient capacity. In the critical phase of their start-up, many of these young companies therefore end up with non-European owners.

On the fiscal side, too, Europe must follow up with further incentives. The multiannual European financial framework and thus the priorities of the European Union continue to be imbalanced in favor of protecting existing industries and especially agriculture, instead of massively increasing investment in growth and research. There are good examples of how common future issues can be tackled in Europe. The research grants given by the European Research Council (ERC) are a particularly good example, whereby internationally recognized top researchers based in Europe can apply for significant research funding. These grants are awarded in a highly competitive process through an elaborate system of assessment by other top researchers and without political interference. This promotes cutting-edge research in Europe and attracts scholars from all over the world to Europe.

So Europe has significant opportunities to take vigorous steps forward in the further development of its existing successful economic model and to create the framework for its companies so that they can survive in the long term against competitors from China and other countries. A stronger state intervention policy, often called for in this context, and a closer connection between state and companies—apparently a lesson learned from the success of the Chinese model—begs an essential question. The answer to this question is, however, of key importance from the perspective of both economic policy and economic theory. Is the Chinese economy successful *because of* its close links to the Chinese state or *despite* these close links? To sum it up in one sentence: the jury is still out.

Notes

1. https://www.spiegel.de/wirtschaft/unternehmen/nur-noch-zwei-deutsche-firmen-sind-unter-den-100-wertvollsten-der-welt-a-1303111.html (accessed January 8, 2020).

2. https://www.ey.com/ch/en/newsroom/news-releases/news-release-ey-swiss-companies-are-becoming-less-attractive-for-chinese-investors (accessed January 8, 2020).

3. https://www.ey.com/Publication/vwLUAssets/ey-chinesische-unternehmenskaeufe-und-beteiligungen-in-europa-august-2019-schweiz/$FILE/ey-chinesische-unternehmenskaeufe-und-beteiligungen-in-europa-august-2019-schweiz.pdf (accessed January 8, 2020).

4. See https://www.spglobal.com/marketintelligence/en/news-insights/trending/masuycwfcn-u4yq878qu-a2 (accessed January 8, 2020).

CHAPTER 15

THE ASIAN CENTURY

IN CONVERSATION WITH PARAG KHANNA

Convoco talked to Parag Khanna about the rise of Asia. Parag Khanna proclaims the 21st century to be the century of Asia after the 20th century was the American and the 19th the European one. He emphasizes that we must find mutually acceptable ways forward. "In all spheres of global life there is a need to graduate from dialogue to synthesis: Western atomism and Eastern holism, humanism and scientific materialism, freedom and harmony, democracy and technocracy."[1]

Convoco: You see technocracy as the future of Asia. Could it be a global future as technologies like AI and big data work in favor of these? China for example has introduced the Social Credit System (SCS). Does this give technocracies a major advantage? Do you think European democracies will be affected?

Parag Khanna: The idea of technocracy is in fact a European idea, and it rests more on the administrative capacity and excellence of the state than on technology per se. But now there is a marriage of data and democracy, the ability to have rapid citizen feedback through elections, surveys, and social media, but also for the government to harness it for more effective citizen engagement and public service delivery. Asians are certainly doing this very well, but so too are Europeans in many countries, especially the smaller ones of the Nordics. China's Social Credit System (SCS) is an example of both the positive and negative applications of big data to governance at the same time.

C: How does Asia deal with what Fukuyama labelled the "Bad emperor problem"? A government with few checks and balances on executive power, like independent courts, a free media or an elected legislature, has amazing power when the emperor is good. But there is also the other side of the coin. The rule of law is one of Europe's core principles. What kind of role does it play for you? Does the West need to change its idea of a "global rules-based order" in favor of the Chinese phrase "community of common destiny", which is preferred by Asians?

PK: Because most European countries today are multi-party parliamentary systems, you do not have the risk of a bad emperor problem as much as the risk of rudderless recycling of ineffective leaders! As for Asia, remember that far more people live in *democracies* in Asia than in authoritarian states. India, Indonesia and the Philippines alone represent 1.8 billion people, which is greater than the population of China. So, let us be clear that in Asia, there are checks on authority in most countries, and most people are not afraid to throw out bad leaders. Indeed, we see how India's Modi and Duterte in the Philippines are struggling in their political campaigns due to their illiberal practices that the people resent. As for global governance, in the book I make clear that the notion of a "global rules-based order" in contrast to a "community of common destiny" is a false choice: they are two sides of the same coin.

C: What does your statement "Asians seek not conquest but respect" imply for the relationship between

Asia and Europe? In your opinion, does Europe have unique strengths on which a long-term strategy should be based? What does it mean to seek respect from the perspective of Asian countries?

PK: Asians largely know from the experience of the Japanese in the 20th century and due to the inherent multipolarity of their vast and diverse system that conquering each other is not possible. They have more of a "live and let live" approach to each other. Europe has innate strengths around democracy, the rule of law, and its highly developed and diversified economies that share the great Eurasian landmass with Asia. They are converging rapidly in trade and infrastructure through the new Silk Roads and I expect this process to accelerate. Europeans must be more unified in their approach to Asia to avoid being divided by China and others in areas of investment and human rights.

C: You emphasize that Asians want economic globalization, not free trade. What is the difference between Asians and Westerners with regard to the market? According to the orthodox capitalist view, growth in itself results in redistribution. For Asians fiscal redistribution drives equitable growth. Is this view mirrored in the recently devised inclusive development index (IDI) that has become the preferred measure of national progress in Asia instead of GDP?

PK: The West no longer represents "free markets" versus an Asian "state capitalism" since in reality the whole world practices some kind of "mixed capitalism" with various roles for the state in the economy. By now everyone should realize that growth alone does not entail adequate redistribution to have an equitable society in an age of financial globalization. The "Inclusive Development Index" (IDI) is a step in the right direction.

C: China has labeled its role in the Asian Security System "peaceful rise" (Hu Jintao) or "harmonious world" (Xi Jinping) indicating that peaceful coexistence and cooperation is mutually beneficial. Prior to World War I Europe had benefited from unprecedented growth and economic integration. Ongoing peaceful cooperation would have been mutually beneficial but the break-down of the balance of power led to war. Do you think that the mainly peaceful cooperation in Asia may be at risk at some point? Which are the most severe areas of tension in your opinion?

PK: I identify at least nine major conflict scenarios for Asia such as Taiwan, Kashmir, North Korea, the South China Sea, and others. Any of these may explode into conflict, but none has so far because Asians have done a good job of balancing their geopolitical tensions with their geoeconomic integration. Furthermore, conflicts in Asia do not necessarily spill over into others in Asia as they have in European history. Asians largely view these situations as isolated from each other. In that sense, even if there are one or more wars in Asia in these situations, there is also a subsequent settlement and continued advance of the Asian system.

Note

1. Parag Khanna, *The Future is Asian* (London: Weidenfeld & Nicolson, 2019), p. 358.

CHAPTER 16

EUROPE AND THE GLOBAL ECONOMIC ORDER

GABRIEL FELBERMAYR

Why do countries voluntarily forego parts of their national sovereignty and subject themselves to international rules and institutions? Clearly, there are benefits from doing so: international cooperation allows a deep division of labor which, in turn, is a crucial determinant of general economic progress. But straightforward observation shows that cooperation has limits: national borders persist and nation states have well-defined parameters.

THE EXAMPLE OF EUROPEAN INTEGRATION

To illustrate the economic logic governing the international integration of markets and institutions, it is useful to consider Europe, still by far the world's most integrated transnational economic space.

Europe has been built around the idea that its Members share a set of fundamental beliefs about the appropriate social and economic order. Only because of this common ground have countries been able to create a Single Market, even a common currency, and the institutions that govern them. Since the beginning, many thinkers expected that national belief systems would converge, gradually giving rise to a distinctive European model. The creation of the Monetary Union is the best example of this hope. However, Brunnermeier, James, and Landau[1] have quite convincingly shown that Europe is still in the middle of a battle of ideas, often along national lines, and that a common way of European thinking is emerging only very slowly. The lack of convergence of ideas is a problem: the more countries differ with respect to their preferences, the more any common set of rules, imposed by some central entity (Brussels), will deviate from the ideal representation of national preferences.

A common way of thinking is not enough to cement a common economic and political institutional framework. Even with a common set of shared beliefs, interests can diverge. European countries differ with respect to their grown institutions, patterns of comparative advantage, and geography. Thus, economic theory quite straightforwardly suggests that the gains from trade differ across countries: small, central countries with comparative advantage in manufacturing benefit more from European integration than larger, peripheral, services-oriented Members. Felbermayr et al.[2] makes this point in a modern quantitative-simulation model for Europe. Britain, it turns out, has benefited the least from the EU. The reason is that it has relatively low trade costs with countries outside the EU (for example because of low language barriers), its own market is the second largest amongst EU Members, and its pattern of comparative advantage implies net exports in the services sectors where the European Single Market is relatively underdeveloped. Hence, the benefits of membership to the EU are lower in the UK than elsewhere.

On top of this, one has to account for heterogeneous preferences, as argued above. But even if countries had perfectly identical preferences, giving away national sovereignty to increase the gains from international market integration comes with a cost: countries that can always be hit by idiosyncratic shocks rationally value the possibility of fine-tuning rules as they see fit. Thus, whether or not to participate in the EU project depends on a trade-off: as long as the gains from further integration outweigh the costs, push ahead; but when the pros no longer outweigh the cons, stop. And, when circumstances change, countries might want to reconsider.

Such a framework can help to identify the limits of a deep European integration project. Moreover, at the global scale, the framework can help explain why some countries are much more inclined to give away national sovereignty to international organizations such as the World Trade Organization (WTO) than others. It appears that lessons learned in Europe are useful when redesigning global governance structures. Most importantly, the European experience suggests that a very complex world probably requires a multi-layered institutional framework such as the one Europe has developed and needs to develop further.

THE WORLD TRADE ORGANIZATION AT 25

On January 1, 1995 the WTO came into existence. It was the result of negotiations during the so-called Uruguay Round which started in 1986 and continued until 1993. In the middle of this period, Soviet-style communism collapsed in Europe. At that time, the attitude was widespread that the Western model of liberal democracies and market economies had won over alternative systems. In 1992 Francis Fukuyama published his famous book titled *The End of History and the Last Man*, expressing the idea that geostrategic rivalry had come to an end and that the future would be one of a single system rather than of systems competition.[3] The WTO extended the Generalized Agreement on Tariffs and Trade (GATT), which had developed from 1948 onwards, and included provisions on services trade (the Generalized Agreement on Trade in Services or GATS) and on the protection of intellectual property. Quite importantly, by contrast with GATT, the WTO has been endowed with an elaborate dispute settlement system.

In many ways, the WTO has been a success story: its membership has grown from 128 essentially non-communist GATT members to 164 countries including former system rivals such as China, Russia,

Vietnam and, of course, almost all formerly communist countries in Europe. It has overseen a period of spectacular expansion in world trade.

However, it has run into an existential crisis. Its appellate body, the appeal "court" of the multilateral system, is no longer functional since, starting under the Obama Administration, the US has refused to confirm the nomination of new judges. The WTO has not been able to conclude any large round of trade negotiations that would bring about a modernization of rules covering digital trade, for example. It has been increasingly made obsolete as an ever-larger share of world trade is covered by preferential trade agreements outside of the WTO.

The WTO suffers from the fact that it has grown very large: it has 164 members of very different economic size, with very different levels of development, and with very different political systems. Establishing, maintaining, modernizing, and enforcing a uniform body of rules for such a heterogeneous collection is obviously challenging. As in the EU, members benefit to varying degrees from the system, and they value the cost of foregoing an unconstrained trade policy quite differently. This suggests that, like Europe, the world needs a multi-layered system that offers distinct models of integration: a deeper one for core members, and a shallower one for the periphery—where periphery is defined in terms of countries' willingness and ability to commit to common rules.

END OF HISTORY NO LONGER

The fundamental issue with the WTO is that the "end-of-history" assumption of the early 1990s is no longer tenable. The period of hyperglobalization[4] that started in the 1990s and endured until 2008, brought about a process of economic convergence in which emerging markets quickly caught up with Western economies, but it has not generated the convergence of political systems hoped for by many. For example, very quickly after China's accession to the WTO in November 2001, China's economy slowed down and later stopped the process of opening up. When, in 2009, the Western world plunged into the deepest recession since World War II, China largely avoided a crisis. Consequently, the West's belief in the superiority of its system, summarized by the Washington Consensus, was shattered while the process of economic convergence quickened dramatically.

Today, the world seems to have returned to a situation of systems competition, where the Western model is challenged by a Chinese alternative that follows not only a different development model but also a very different philosophy regarding the relationship between state and economy. What is more, the largest "Western" economy, the US, is in the process of being overtaking in size by its "Eastern" rival.

The problem is that the WTO has not been designed for such an environment. Its central tenet is that all its members have the same fundamental objective, i.e. to maximize their citizens' per capita income. Under this assumption, the WTO's principles of reciprocity and non-discrimination have been shown by economists Kyle Bagwell and Robert Staiger to yield a stable cooperative equilibrium, despite the short-run temptation of beggar-thy-neighbor policies.[5] Cooperation generates welfare gains everywhere. In the absence of geostrategic rivalry, it does not matter that the gains are distributed unevenly, typically in favor of poorer countries.

But when geostrategic competition enters the picture, countries increasingly care about the size of their own economies relative to their rivals'. This would be irrelevant in "end-of-history" thinking. Unfortunately, the Bagwell–Staiger results no longer hold in the presence of geostrategic considerations: reciprocity and non-discrimination no longer yield the right incentives for countries to foreswear the use of tariffs and non-cooperative trade policies. Rather, they may use trade policy instruments to keep geostrategic rivals at bay. In other words, the WTO and GATT were designed to bring about cooperative outcomes in positive-sum games. This worked well between 1948 and 1990, when the system applied almost exclusively to US allies and excluded the Soviet Union and its satellites, and for the first years thereafter, when the "end-of-history" thinking prevailed. But the WTO and GATT rules have problems operating when countries fear domination and abuse by others. Such a configuration is inherently zero-sum in nature. In economic history, times of system competition are associated with block building and the weaponization of tariffs.[6]

The founding father of modern economics, Adam Smith, already described this problem in his 1776 magnum opus *The Wealth of Nations*. After praising the advantages of an international division of labor and warning against the economic costs of beggar-thy-neighbor policies, in Book IV he defends the Navigation Acts—a set of policies that had the objective of keeping Dutch sailors out of British harbors using the famous formulation "defence, however, is of much more importance than opulence".[7] The British regarded the Dutch as geostrategic rivals who could not be trusted: the expectation was that they would recklessly exploit

British competitors if they were allowed to dominate global maritime trade links. Without sufficient trust, that a deep global division of labor does not lead to exploitation by a trade partner whenever it has the opportunity, such security concerns appear of vital national interest.

Indeed, GATT contains a national security exception in its Article XXI, and Section 232 of the 1962 US Trade Expansion Act enables the US President to impose tariffs on imports that threaten national security. In March 2018, citing these legal texts, the US imposed tariffs on steel and aluminum products, including on exports from NATO allies such as the UK or Germany. It is very hard to defend the US argument in this case, but the existence of those instruments both in international and in US law shows that Smith's qualification has always been important for lawmakers.

By contrast, economists, at least in mainstream thinking, have tended to ignore these considerations, probably for both positive and normative reasons. First, the global economy of the post-World War II period was so clearly dominated by the US that one could safely design optimal institutions within the given power system and ignore security considerations. Second, economists were understandably reluctant to advocate aggressive policies that would harm the world economy. As a consequence, political security considerations are almost fully absent in the economic analysis of commercial policy.[8]

WAR BY OTHER MEANS

Political thinkers have been less reluctant. Robert Blackwill and Jennifer Harris show how a large, technologically advanced country such as the US can successfully engage in "war by other means."[9] In such a context, the success of commercial policies is not (only) measured by their consequences on per capita income but also and maybe predominantly by their effects on one country's GDP relative to another's.

To understand the present condition of the global trading system one has to account for the geostrategic picture. Even before the current US President came to power, the US was working on strategies to contain the economic rise of China. The Transpacific Partnership (TPP) agreement designed by Secretary of State Clinton intended to marginalize China; studies predicting its economic consequences show this quite clearly.[10] The current US administration very explicitly uses trade policy tools to slow down economic progress in China. Indeed, most empirical studies of the ongoing trade conflict suggest that the economic damage of the mutual imposition of tariffs is at least three times larger in absolute terms in China than in the US. So, when US President Trump tweets that trade wars are good and easy to win,[11] he might be right if success is measured in a zero-sum game in which the winning party is the one that inflicts the larger economic costs on its rival.

A RISKY STRATEGY

But trade wars do generate economic damage, on both sides of the conflict, and for the world economy as a whole. And the danger of economic damage extends beyond tariffs. Since 2009 the use of other measures aimed at protecting markets against foreign competition has gone up systematically. The rise of non-tariff measures over the last ten years has been documented.[12] In many ways, they are worse than tariffs. First, they are much less transparent—their costs are less obvious as they are often cleverly disguised as legitimate regulation; second, they do not generate tariff income but impose often wasteful extra expenditure on trade partners; third, the international rules offer fewer ways of dealing with them. Examples are easily found in procurement regulation such as the Buy American Act, competition law, taxation, and even in fiscal stimulus programs such as the Car Allowance Rebate System (also known as "cash for clunkers.")

While their economic costs are higher than tariffs, non-tariff measures can also be used to pursue geostrategic objectives. Finally, uncertainty about the conditions of market access can be used strategically as well. The threat of a tariff might be enough to induce foreign producers to serve a large market by local production rather than by exports. More generally, in an increasingly unpredictable world, large economies tend to appear as safe havens. Such countries may therefore have incentives to generate uncertainty.

Clearly, such strategies are very risky. Economic history teaches important lessons. After the US had imposed high tariffs on trade partners under the 1930 Smoot–Hawley Tariff Act and other countries had reciprocated, world trade spiraled from $5.3 billion to just $1.8 billion in 1933. Economic historians largely agree that those tariffs did not cause the Great Recession but they prolonged it, thereby paving the way for the atrocities of World War II.

SLOWBALIZATION

As a consequence of the return of trade restrictions, international trade growth has slowed down. Trade is still expanding as the world economy grows, but its growth rate relative to total production has declined. During the era of hyperglobalization, trade in goods expanded much faster than industrial production: countries imported an increasing share of domestic demand and exported an increasing share of domestic production. Since approximately 2008, goods trade no longer outperforms production; the process of globalization has come to a stop.

The OECD Trade in Value-Added statistics show that since about 2010 global value chains have started shortening in many countries, most strongly in China. In 2000 one dollar's worth of Chinese exports contained 40 cents of foreign value added in the form of foreign inputs; by 2015 that share had fallen to 17 cents.[13]

It is still debated to what extent the rise of protectionism since 2009 relative to other forces such as a fundamental change in the Chinese growth model has contributed to this phenomenon that the British magazine *The Economist* has called "slowbalization." It is also unclear how the situation outside of goods trade, which still dominates international trade statistics, has evolved. International services transactions and data flows continue to grow, but there are severe measurement issues and the performance of international transactions relative to domestic ones is not straightforward to ascertain.

Having said this, technological change is likely to have important effects on the integration of the world economy. Over the last 70 years, technological changes such as the introduction of containerization or the digitalization of the supply chain have had stronger effects on the growth of trade relative to domestic transactions than policy has. Hence, it is probably safe to assume that further innovations, such as artificial intelligence, will lead to a further reduction in trade costs, for example in the need for expensive language translation. For this reason, the American economist Richard Baldwin expects a new wave of globalization that might go deeper into the fabric of national labor markets than former waves.[14] At the same time, new technologies might lead to the reshoring of production from labor-rich emerging markets back to capital-rich ones.

WHAT IS TO BE DONE? FIVE IDEAS FOR THE NEW EU COMMISSION

Despite these uncertainties, and for the reasons sketched at the beginning of this essay, it is clear that slowbalization is more painful for some countries than for others. Germany, for instance, is more vulnerable than any other industrialized country with a similarly sized domestic market.[15] Europe as a whole also appears more vulnerable than either the US or China. On top of this, the EU has no offensive geostrategic interests such as the US or China do, but it still risks being drawn into their conflict. It is all too easily imaginable that a US administration might ask for European support in its conflict with China, leaving the old continent an extremely difficult choice between losing either the US or the Chinese market while maintaining the other.

For the new European Commission under its President Ursula von der Leyen, there are five points of strategic importance that emerge from the analysis conducted above.

First and foremost, in a world of new geostrategic rivalry and systems competition, where key players are driven by zero-sum reasoning, Europe must ask itself what its own interests are and how it can defend them. It is of paramount importance to recognize that the global order has changed and will not return to the friendly ecosystem led by the US from after World War II to, say, 2006, that was so conducive to the construction of the European project. The European project always had the objective of promoting European economic sovereignty: the Customs Union, the Single Market, and the Monetary Union all exist because the EU Members are much better able to defend their interests in a coalition than they could each on their own. This is why they have given up independent trade policy, regulatory autonomy, and their own currencies.

In the new era of geostrategic rivalry, the EU risks losing out if it does not develop further. In particular, it needs to define an appropriate concept of economic sovereignty, and develop its related objectives and instruments. The historical focus of the EU on economics rather than on security and national defense needs to be reconsidered, but without naïveté: in this context, as with economic integration, benefits need to outweigh costs, and the latter tend to be larger in the multi-country European Union than in any classical nation state. This means that, first, economics will continue to play a pivotal role, and second, the EU needs to learn how to use its economic clout to achieve its strategic goals.

The danger, of course, is that under the pretext of defending its economic sovereignty, the EU turns towards downright protectionism. Therefore, any sharpened or newly developed instruments, such as for example the EU investment screening regulation, must come with mechanisms that insulate them against protectionist abuse. Any new instrument must be generalizable to a desirable multilateral order—which, however, does not mean that it must necessarily comply with the WTO, the 25-year-old institution developed, as explained above, under the now defunct "end-of-history" paradigm. Whenever possible, the EU should proceed with like-minded allies, with whom free trade agreements exist or are in the process of being concluded, such as Canada, Japan, Korea, Australia, and so forth. Also, the EU should avoid new illusions such as the idea that the diffusion of technology could be blocked. We live in a globalized world and, even with new political barriers, the flow of ideas will continue.

Second, and central to developing a strategy to defend its economic sovereignty, the EU must do whatever it can to defend and further deepen its Single Market. It is by far the most valuable ingredient of the EU integration project: 75 percent or more of the welfare gains from the EU originate here.[16] The Single Market is the best possible insurance device: when the international order crumbles and new uncertainties build up, it serves as a safe haven for European producers, consumers, and workers. It increases the gains that Member States have accrued from being in the EU and therefore reduces centrifugal forces. Access to it is the EU's most important asset in international negotiations. A deep and successful Single Market gives the EU external clout. For these reasons, the EU must prioritize the establishment of a common digital market, common energy and electricity markets, the development of adequate infrastructure to underpin those ambitions, and the willingness to further develop transnational transportation links. It also must repair the Schengen Zone and end border controls within it. Survey evidence put forward by various sources shows that frictions in the Single Market have increased, not fallen, therefore compromising the EU's strategic interests.[17]

The withdrawal of Britain from the EU is, of course, a big blow to the EU's international influence. Brexit reduces the size of the Single Market in a way equivalent to the exit of the 19 smallest EU Members. Therefore, Europe must work out models that tie countries on the European periphery—such as post-Brexit Britain, Turkey, or Switzerland—to the Single Market as strongly as possible. Crucially, Europe should offer countries, which are not in the European Union proper, entry into a customs association. While such an agreement would not go as deep as the EU Single Market, it could fully cover goods markets. At least in this area, then, the EU would maintain or even extend its international reach.

The third area of importance in defending economic sovereignty relates to the Monetary Union. In many countries, the Euro is seen almost exclusively as a monetary policy project. As a consequence, the discussion is almost always about flows of credits between central banks (target balances), interest rates, or quantitative easing. Sometimes, trade economists stress that the Euro is also about transaction costs. They show that the introduction of the Euro has indeed fostered trade between its Members.[18]

The Euro is, however, too rarely thought of as a geostrategic tool. This could mean striking compromises in the area of monetary policy. For example, to increase the Euro's role as an international reserve currency, a sufficiently large supply of safe Euro denominated bonds is of paramount importance. This could be achieved by creating European Safe Bonds (ESBies).

The fourth area of action is international trade policy. The WTO as the cornerstone of the multilateral order is in an existential crisis. As explained above, that crisis relates to very fundamental issues arising from systems competition that will not go away any time soon. For this reason, the EU needs to develop a "Plan B." It has already concluded an agreement with Canada about a substitute to the appellate body; it needs to develop this further and extend it to as many countries as possible. More generally, Europe needs to prepare for a world in which the WTO might suffer even more damage than it already has. For example, Article XXI, which allows members to cite national security concerns to suspend trade concessions, is already more widely applied, substantially increasing trade policy uncertainty around the world. Europe needs to do more to defend the key elements of the multilateral order, and, if necessary, apply more pressure.

This, however, requires credibility. Europe must move beyond paying lip service. It has followed Trump's steel tariffs by imposing its own steel tariffs against third countries such as Brazil, Turkey, or South Korea, in order to avoid their steel products being redirected into Europe. I think this is a mistake. We need a club of the willing—countries that want to protect the WTO. The WTO has 164 members; the US is one and China is another, but there are 162 more. Many of them are looking for leadership. Europe should provide this leadership—who else could?—and play a constructive role in modernizing the WTO, in making it greener and more flexible, but without pretending to maintain a single model that works uniformly for all countries.

Finally, Europe has to be more confident in the value of bilateral trade agreements. True, a global set of rules is preferable to bilateral agreements that tend to generate harmful trade diversion and fragment the trading system. But if the global system is breaking down and legal certainty is becoming weaker, bilateral agreements are welcome remedies. Therefore, Europe needs to develop additional and deeper bilateral trade agreements that cover more countries and more areas. Again, compromises will be needed. For example, the Mercosur agreement or those with ASEAN countries do come with the risk of generating inconsistencies in the area of environmental policy. But safeguarding transparency and legal order in an increasingly disorderly global trading system would be a very important achievement indeed.

Notes

1. Markus K. Brunnermeier, Harold James, and Jean-Pierre Landau, *The Euro and the Battle of Ideas* (Princeton: Princeton University Press, 2016).

2. Gabriel Felbermayr, Jasmin Gröschl, and Inge Heiland, "Undoing Europe in a New Quantitative Trade Model," ifo Working Paper Series 250 (ifo Institute, Leibniz Institute for Economic Research at the University of Munich, 2018).

3. Francis Fukuyama, *The End of History and the Last Man* (New York: Free Press, 1992).

4. Dani Rodrik, *The Globalization Paradox: Democracy and the Future of the World Economy* (New York: W. W. Norton & Co, 2011).

5. Kyle Bagwell and Robert W. Staiger, *The Economics of the World Trading System* (Cambridge, MA: The MIT Press, 2002).

6. Douglas A. Irwin, *Against the Tide: An Intellectual History of Free Trade* (Princeton, NJ: Princeton University Press, 1998).

7. Adam Smith, *An Inquiry into the Nature and Causes of the Wealth of Nations* (London: W. Strahan and T. Cadell, 1776), p. 465.

8. For example, see the chapters in Kyle Bagwell and Robert W. Staiger (eds.), *Handbook of Commercial Policy* (Amsterdam: North Holland, 2016).

9. Robert D. Blackwill and Jennifer M. Harris, *War by Other Means: Geoeconomics and Statecraft* (Cambridge, MA: Harvard University Press, 2016).

10. Rahel Aichele and Gabriel Felbermayr, *The Trans-Pacific Partnership Deal (TPP): What are the Economic Consequences*

for In- and Outsiders? GED Focus Paper (Bertelsmann Foundation, 2015).

11. Tweet by @realDonaldTrump, March 2, 2018.

12. Simon Evenett, and Johannes Fritz, *Jaw, Jaw not War, War: Prioritising WTO Reform Options*, The 24th Global Trade Alert Report (London: CEPR Press, 2019).

13. OECD, "Trade in Value-Added Database," 2018, https://www.oecd.org/sti/ind/measuring-trade-in-value-added.htm (accessed December 10, 2019).

14. Richard Baldwin, *The Globotics Upheaval: Globalization, Robotics, and the Future of Work* (Oxford: Oxford University Press, 2019).

15. Here, it is important to distinguish between Germany as a country with immobile citizens, and German firms that might be active in many countries and therefore able to hedge against trade policy uncertainty.

16. Gabriel Felbermayr, Jasmin Gröschl, and Inge Heiland, "Undoing Europe in a New Quantitative Trade Model," ifo Working Paper Series 250 (ifo Institute, Leibniz Institute for Economic Research at the University of Munich, 2018).

17. For example, DIHK-Deutscher Industrie und Handelskammertag, *DIHK Survey on Single Market Obstacles* (Berlin, 2019).

18. Gabriel Felbermayr and Marina Steininger, "Revisiting the Euro's Trade Costs and Welfare Effects" in *Journal of Economics and Statistics* 239 (5–6), pp. 917–956.

CHAPTER 17

THE END OF AN ERA, THE BEGINNING OF A NEW: STRUCTURAL CHANGE IN THE EUROPEAN ECONOMY

FREDRIK ERIXON

THE END OF AN ERA

The European economy, just like the global economy, is changing: we are currently moving from one era to another. These fundamental economic changes are also accompanied by political disruption in the West. It is easy to identify the political turbulence because it is constantly part of the news cycle. However, it is not as if Donald Trump or anyone else has suddenly broken an old structure apart and ushered us into chaos or uncertainty. Rather, we have lived through gradual shifts in the postwar economic order, and those shifts started long before the arrival of Donald Trump in the White House or the disruption of European politics.

Let us start by outlining the shifts in economic policy. For several decades, a guiding principle of international economic policy—inside as well as outside Europe—was to reduce the role of government in shaping the course of the economy. Obviously, governments kept a tight grip on some aspects of economic policy; for instance, they have exerted influence on the economy through taxes and government spending regardless of the prevailing ideological moods. But the policy framework that emerged after the crises of the 1960s and 1970s intended to establish rules for policy and make it more predictable. Trade and monetary policy are a case in point.

In Europe, the creation of the Common Market and, later, the Single Market created institutions and rules that reduced the space for government discretion. While there was still a policy in place, these market rules were directly motivated by the desire to have predictable and fair rules, and to avoid the consequences of the discretionary power structures that had existed before.

In the past, policies had all too often been made up along the way and they routinely led governments to hand out privileges and advantages to some entrepreneurs and companies, but not to others. There was a degree of unfairness in policy. Perhaps more importantly, the centrality of governments with discretionary power led economic operators to concentrate too much of their time on wooing officialdom.

Central banks were largely a domain of secrecy. They too were often guided by various schools of thought, but it was principally impossible for the outside world to have an idea of the long-term ambition of their policy. Therefore, in the 1980s, many central banks moved to a policy that aimed at predictability. Inflation control became the paramount goal. Central banks were made independent to avoid undue political influence. They also opened up to create more transparency and started to publish their long-term forecasts for inflation and interest rates. In other words, monetary policy was shaped by rules rather than discretion.

This new direction of trade and monetary policy was part of the old era, an era that was also underpinned by other economic factors. Most parts of the Western hemisphere had a period with a benign demographic situation in the sense that the working population could, with relative ease, support people who were not in employment. This also included providing government support to the growing educational sector and allowing young people to delay entry into the labor force.

The demographics also helped the growth of the international economy. From the 1960s and a couple of decades thereafter, big cohorts entered the labor force and gave firms opportunities to scale up without labor shortage problems. The growth of female labor led to a huge expansion in the economy's labor supply. For several decades, the economy was able to grow through the addition of new production factors.

International trade also boomed, mainly in manufacturing and consumer goods. That type of trade gradually became global. While it started being more transatlantic and perhaps more European, it expanded geographically and in due course included many of the emerging markets that have now gained prominence in the world economy. Cross-border trade and investment became forces of economic convergence in the world.

This old era also had other characteristics. One was the process of cultural denationalization—a liberal norm where we gradually expanded the spheres of loyalties to include those outside our national borders. Nation-state borders were no longer natural demarcations for culture and identity. Instead, people became gradually preoccupied with the health and welfare of people who lived outside their own national territories. Cultural internationalism led many to become more interested in foreign cultures and less interested in national traditions and local cultural identity.

Moreover, the old era was also characterized by the acceptance of technocratic global governance. Electorates accepted the transfer of sovereignty to institutions outside national borders and outside national structures of legitimacy and authority. International institutions such as the World Trade Organization (WTO) expanded their scope and influence on national decision-making. European integration accelerated.

Finally, there was visionary generosity in power politics and global politics, especially on the part of America, the hegemonic power for a good part of this era. US administrations supported the growth of other economies, even if over time that growth would undermine American power. The US accepted that other countries would not open their markets to the same degree as they did because they believed that the process of economic openness would continue nevertheless and eventually generate more benefits for the US economy.

For instance, Europe received strong support from America when it was rebuilding its economies and societies after World War II. There was American support for China to join the World Trade Organization in 2001, despite America knowing that WTO accession would boost China's growth and eventually make the Chinese economy larger than the US economy.

THE BEGINNING OF A NEW ERA

We are now at the beginning of a new era. The rules, institutions, and norms of the old era are still with us, and are likely to remain with us for quite some time. Hopefully they will not die, but many of them are now withering away.

Discretionary economic authority and decision-making is now returning. As a consequence, economic policy is becoming less predictable. Central banking is now dominated by discretion rather than rules. The motivations for these changes can be debated, but it is clear that monetary policy has been undergoing a process of innovation and it is difficult for the outside world to understand its *modus operandi*. If the past decades aimed to make monetary policy discretion less influential on the rest of the economy, we are now back in a situation where decisions by central banks have a huge influence on the real economy and financial markets.

Trade policy has changed too. It was thought that old issues such as tariffs had become obsolete, but they are now part of growing trade frictions between different parts of the world. The US is led by a President who is on record saying he likes trade wars.

Nor is the demographic outlook favorable. Many Western societies, plus other nations such as China and Japan, have a difficult demographic balance with a high portion of the population in retirement, low rates of childbirth, or both. As a consequence, there is growing competition for resources—especially government resources—between generations that make claims on the public purse. There is also resource competition between countries, especially for tax revenues. Every country now wants to poach more tax revenues from global firms. If they do not get as much in tax revenue as they think they should, they look for other means to obtain it. For instance, France and other European countries are now introducing a sales tax on digital services, with the purpose of taxing corporate income they think they are missing out on because of unfair international rules on corporate income tax.

Economic globalization is also moving into a new era. The process of cross-border economic integration is continuing, but it is now driven by new flows. The growth in global trade in goods has stalled. While it used to grow twice as fast as global economic growth, global goods trade now grows at half the rate of economic growth—in a good year. However, the trade in services is growing and—importantly—trade in digital services has boomed (see Chart 1).

Chart 1: Growth in Global Trade

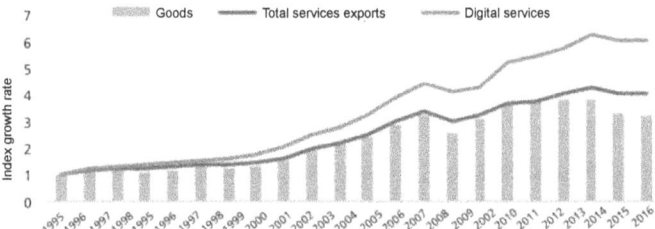

The new foundation of cross-border integration is digital, and obviously this reflects the fact that the economy in general is increasingly going digital. The digital economy is basically constituted by knowledge, human capital, R&D, innovation, and new technology. The good news is that all these factors are difficult to stop at the border. If someone in San Francisco comes up with a brilliant idea, it is very difficult to stop that person from sharing that idea with someone in Salzburg or with someone in another part of the world. And it is predominantly ideas that will drive economic integration in the new era.

Two other points about the new era merit attention. The first one is the rediscovery of national identity. It is unclear where this trend is going, but it seems to be a defining aspect of current political turbulence in the West. It manifests itself in different ways. For some, the quest for national identity is inclusive and not a wholesale refutation of global cooperation. For others, it is based on notions about shared ancestry and—often—expressed in ethnic terms, for example white nationalism.

Either way, a good part of Europe and America is increasingly interested in protecting patterns of loyalty that are national rather than international. As a consequence, there is growing skepticism about the principles and norms that defined much of the internationalist ambitions of the old era, leading some to question international trade, migration, or the European Union. Nor is it a uniquely Western trait. China is on a clear path of exclusive and Han-dominated nationalism. Asia in general is organizing itself according to a pattern of "Eastphalia"—similar to Europe's "Westphalian" culture of state and identity, where nationalism and national identity are constituent parts of a new type of modernity, clearly different from the liberal modernity that became dominant in the post-1989 world.

Perhaps we are also seeing the Europeanization of America. The US was founded on a different idea from European nations and has always been a melting pot for various cultures. Its common and cognitive unifier has been the federalist constitution, not a national language or a national religion. The America that is emerging now is less confident about its old arrangement. There is a growth of opinions in America that is seeking to define the country as a nation with a shared language, religion, ancestry, culture, and identity.

The second point is the growing occupation of redressing perceived injustices in global relations. Many emerging economies are now intent on reclaiming a global role that they think others have deprived them of. Equally, the US President and others in America are increasingly incensed, identifying their grievances with other countries and correcting bilateral relations they believe to have been disadvantageous to the country. Trade agreements with other countries, such as NAFTA and the US–Korea Free Trade Agreement, have been seen by the US leadership as opportunities for foreigners to rip-off US workers. The US administration is seeking trade confrontations with China on the basis of the same type of rhetoric: China is taking advantage of America. A good part of America's policy in the Middle East is now driven by grievances and perceptions of unfair treatment of the US.

In conclusion, the world that we are entering is a world which is going to be much less predictable. It is not a world of deglobalization or where we return to autarkic types of economic systems without cross-border trade and investment. Arguably, the digital economy is going to keep up the pace of global exchange. However, international economics and politics will be less guided by rules and institutions. National power will become more present and relevant for shaping relations and settling disputes. There will be a larger space for discretionary economic authority.

THE FATE OF EUROPE

Where will Europe find itself in this era? And how will it fare in a world defined by structural economic changes, the growth of the ideas-based economy, not least through rapid digitalization of goods production as well as services production? There is not one single answer. The structural economic transformation in Europe, for example, is varied. Europe features huge variations between countries and between regions within countries; some countries are at the frontier of new innovative growth, while others are struggling to catch up.

However, the average European performance is not as good as it should be, and in particular the digital transformation is comparatively slow. The good news is that Europe has succeeded in improving its digital infrastructure. Even if Europe as a region is trailing behind other regions in 5G investments for example, Europe has rapidly grown its digital endowments and its network capacity. Digital human capital has also gone up substantially.

The bad news is that these investments have not much improved the digital intensity of Europe's growth. When Europe is compared to other relevant parts of the world, it is clear that they are using their endowments to generate more output. They have a higher intensity of economic output from these endowments. And the problem is that too many firms and operators are too slow to adapt to new technology and new ways of doing business. Europe's information and communications technology (ICT) and software sector is thriving, but the problem is that too many non-ICT sectors have been slow in bringing technologies into their own firms and powering their own growth with it.

The final point is that European governments have failed to build a single market that is adapted to the type of economy that will dominate the new era. In fact, there is now a disassociation between the EU Single Market and European economic development, for the simple reason that structural transformation of the economy is moving us away from a goods-dominated economy to a services and digital intensities economy. And when it comes to services and the digital economy, Europe is not as well integrated as it is in the goods-based economy. Key policies for market access in the digital economy are lacking in the EU and there is substantial heterogeneity among the EU membership in the approaches they are taking.

As a consequence, Europe is struggling to make itself relevant as a leader of global economic affairs in the new era. While it has established rules on privacy and data integrity that other countries are now imitating, few look to Europe for leadership in how markets can be opened up in order to spur faster innovation and high-quality growth. Unless Europe can turn this development around and establish itself in the vanguard of the market rules and institutions that will guide the 21st-century economy, it will also find that the rest of the world will become less interested in Europe's position and contributions in other areas.

CHAPTER 18

ON THE VALUE OF EUROPE'S DIVERSITY

CHRISTOPH G. PAULUS

A. GLOBAL: THE QUEST FOR UNITY

E pluribus unum—the US has managed to create "out of many, one" in the form of the United States of America. Europe did not succeed—and has no intention of doing so. Rather, Europe's motto is "Unity in diversity," thus emphasizing the differences. While the US has had its slogan for almost two and a half centuries, blazing it abroad on every one-dollar bill in an eye-catching way, Europe only selected its motto via a school competition some two decades ago. So we might infer from this fact that today's European Union is, as it were, concealing its original starting point after the end of World War II and the attendant endeavor to create peace in this for centuries, if not millennia, war-torn territory. The primary goal was not to create unity, but rather peace.

Then we come to China, the third player on the world stage. China has no need of mottos to prove its understanding of unity; it has, as it were, grown over a thousand years of history and has been completely internalized. For even if today's China started out fragmented into several, small empires, unlike Europe it has not remained stuck in multi-nationalism. Rather, the theaters of internecine war that were originally pursued intensively and persistently in China were subdued in 221 BCE after a painfully long time upon the victory of the King of Qin, who as Qin Shi Huang founded the Qin Dynasty and united the empire. This transition to a unitary state is dramatized in director Zhang Yimou's 2002 movie *Hero* in an aesthetically superlative and thematically impressive style.

B. GLOBAL: THREATS TO UNITY

These three very different unities were, of course, threatened time and again. As far as the United States is concerned, the most striking and serious threat was the American Civil War in the era of Abraham Lincoln, that is in the mid 19th century, which had become necessary to prevent the nation dividing in two. However, the victory of the North and with it the condemnation of slavery was not able to suppress the issue of race once and for all, with the result that even today segregation still poses a potential threat that could explode at any time. In that respect, the ostentatiously hoisted *Unum* can be likened to a carpet beneath which serious tensions concerning plurality are swept. The fact that these tensions are currently being fueled (or even increased) rather than combated by the current administration requires no further comment or examples.

Threats to unity in China simmered for nearly two millennia, principally in the North. Of course, even here internal unity was repeatedly threatened by intense and prolonged power struggles between the old subsidiary kingdoms. Nevertheless, the enormity of the Great Wall of China shows that the Mongols had been identified as the main threat. Yet in the 13th century CE, Genghis Khan succeeded in conquering the Chinese in spite of the Wall, and his grandson, Kublai Khan, even managed to found the Yuan dynasty there. This was—and still is today—perceived as oppressive and shameful foreign rule, just like the Qing dynasty, which began about 400 years later, and which was made up of the Manchu ruling elite. This nomadic people also did not let the Wall, which had in the meantime even been extended, prevent them from besieging and defeating the last rulers of the Ming dynasty and establishing a new social, cultural, and political system in China. What was lost as a result of this and the earlier foreign rule may well have been preserved in the multidimensional complexity of the book known to every modern Chinese citizen, namely the *Dream of the Red Chamber* (also called the *Story of the Stone*).

The Europeans were the last to conquer China. Today they are only gradually beginning to realize that China's present-day behavior is also a result of this experience. This also includes the quite panicky (over-) reaction to Taiwan's actual or assumed efforts towards autonomy or, more recently in fall 2019, those of Hong Kong and the Uighurs. Such reactions highlight the extent to which China's ruling echelons fear any threat to uniformity.

Europe's unity is only very recent and therefore, because of a lack of sufficient time to bed in, it is especially fragile. That turns the Euro crisis and is currently turning the Brexit crisis into a particularly dangerous concoction, since what was painstakingly cemented by the Treaties of Rome is unwieldy and freighted with severe legacy burdens created by a centuries-old prehistory of war and conflict. Whatever the cause, or at least what appeared to be a somewhat credible cause, over the centuries this has provided a welcome opportunity to take up arms once again and fight for supremacy in Europe or just against each other.[1]

But the differences that define the divisions between the European states and peoples go even deeper and transcend the persistent, latent readiness for war. In order to identify this, we have to go far back in history and look at things from a distance. In his book *The Silk Roads*, Peter Frankopan draws attention to the fact that our established, singular "Silk Road" is only now through the Chinese concept of the "New Silk Road" becoming plural, thus almost completely ignoring the actual circumstances of the last two millennia or more. Looking at the entire continent of Eurasia during this period, we realize not only that the economic and cultural center lay almost entirely in the Far East, but also that there were almost continuous intensive trade and travel routes from East to West—the West being not the continent of Europe or even its center, but rather Russia, Persia, and possibly the eastern Mediterranean region. One of Frankopan's central theses is that European historiography has dramatically misunderstood the main global regions of action, which has led to a distortion in perspective.

Be that as it may, one of these Silk Roads was established by the aforementioned Genghis Khan in the mid 13th century. And on this route, and that of his successors, it was not so much a question of cultivating and promoting trade as of brutal subjugation and one-sided appropriation. Genghis Khan's triumphant advance was so sweeping that the rulers and peoples of what constitutes modern-day Europe lived in complete fear and the deepest terror. And it is only thanks to the attractiveness and legendary fame of the Persian Empire that the unfettered advance of the Mongol army did not carry straight on through Poland and beyond to Germany, France, England or Italy, but instead turned south.

If, in light of this historical review, we put ourselves in the position of the Europeans of that time, the situation must have been terrible. The rumor that the "scourge of humanity" was approaching in the shape of Genghis Khan and his followers, and that no one could successfully withstand this onslaught, spread like lightning throughout all of Europe and must have caused panic, as did the Ottoman siege of Vienna a few centuries later. Indeed, there arose the quite realistic threat that people would be forced into the Atlantic Ocean and thrown over the cliffs of the world where they would perish miserably.

Both manifestly and surprisingly, however, this imaginary version of past events was not entirely in accordance with what actually happened. For the obvious course of events—obvious because it is psychologically so immediately reasonable and observable again and again in history and world politics—that the common enemy from the outside brings together even deeply divided parties and enables them to make common cause against said external enemy, did not take place. In fact, the reverse happened: at precisely this moment, France and England took the liberty of starting a war that lasted well over one hundred years. The Margraviate of Brandenburg, Bohemia, and the Lithuanians even took possession of areas of Poland which had, in turn, been weakened by defeat and the subsequent ongoing threat of the Mongols themselves. But even the two sieges of Vienna by the Ottomans, thus once again something resembling a common external enemy, were unable to bring the European peoples together. Rather, this was accomplished a long time later in the first half of the 20th century, and after a myriad of more bloody wars, when the (German) enemy within was subsequently contained, and included in a set of treaties out of which the European Union developed.

In this short and cursory historical recap, it should have become sufficiently clear that European unity is more a premise than a lived reality. It must be won and therefore requires constant and sustained effort. How intense this effort must be is shown once again by the seemingly banal example of a basic question: what answer would a European give to the question posed by a non-European when asked to provide a concise explanation of what constitutes European unity, or what common bond exists among Europeans?

In itself the question brings us up short; and the search for an answer requires deep reflection. Perhaps, historically speaking, reference could be made to the Judeo-Christian tradition or, in a more secular way, to the Western tradition. Unlike Asian cultures at least, we might also refer to the emphasis on the individual, which has been cultivated in philosophical and juristic thought literally for millennia. Urban architecture might also provide a suitable answer. If we compare small university towns in Japan, the US, and Europe, we will see that their main squares convey different ideals. Typically, the European square places church, town hall and university in proximity, and are each positioned along the sightline of the ruler's palace. Whether it's Heidelberg, Aix-en-Provence, Coimbra, Urbino, Wrocław, or Oxford, their respective footprints resemble each other more closely than for example, those of Berkeley or Fukuoka.

C. EUROPE: DIVERSITY AS AN OPPORTUNITY

In other words, there are indeed certainly similarities, but the divergences seem to dominate. And yet it does not necessarily follow from the probably undeniable evidence that we must necessarily see this as a disadvantage; for these divergences are at least sometimes also associated with definite advantages, which are absolutely and especially noticeable by comparison with the two other great players in contemporary world affairs.

Surprisingly, this is particularly powerful in a comparison with the US when looking at the economic data of everyday life.[2] For example, cell phone use in the US currently costs around $80 per month; in Germany, however, it costs around €15. Less dramatically, a basket of everyday food in Germany still costs around 50 percent less than US prices. The reason for this may be the increasing concentration and thus the size and associated market power of the companies involved.[3] This is all the more surprising as, more than 100 years ago, the US—with its Sherman Antitrust Act of 1890—was the undisputed champion of legally binding and sanctioned controls on corporate mergers, and thus of controls on competition-suppressing market concentration. Decades later, after World War II, it was this legal system that emerged as the guiding principle of the economic insights that as competition dwindles consumer prices rise and that competition must therefore be preserved, a principle adopted by the Western world and subsequently almost the entire globe. It appears that the author of this principle has forgotten their own teachings, and that European students at least have taken on board these lessons.

One of the explanations for this amazing phenomenon is none other than the European Union (EU). Groaning under the divergences of the Member States and giving the British a welcome pretext for their withdrawal through its lack of democratic legitimacy, this entity with its much-maligned Commission enforces competition restrictions, of which its former role model is apparently no longer capable. The

Democratic presidential candidate Elizabeth Warren, for example, stresses, however, that such restrictions must be imposed upon the market giants of the modern digital economy. It works in the EU because here an ambiguous game is being played and can be played. Individual states can wash their hands in ostensible innocence and shift onto the officials in "Brussels" responsibility for the massive cartel fines, the rigorous prosecution of unfair competition, and for breaking up markets that are too close-knit.

Moreover, this "Brussels" is a monster that is more difficult to crack than, for example, a national domestic ministry, as the commissioners are not answerable to one but to 27 governments. It is not really feasible for a commissioner to operate unilaterally on behalf of his or her nation state, because it might provoke others to take similar action. Political common sense coupled with reciprocal resentment or long-internalized mistrust suddenly leads to effective mutual control, and self-restraint. Moreover, on the one hand in this remarkably hierarchical system the strategy known as "regulatory capture" is considerably hindered—to undermine the regulators, as it were. Access to the decisive European institutions is governed by laws and regulations that differ from those governing the relationship between the domestic industry and the domestic regulator. On the other hand, the fact that the Strasbourg Parliament is comprised of many states makes it difficult to buy influence. As a result, for example, the EU Competition Directorate is more independent than the US Federal Trade Commission. Campaign donations have a much more direct effect in the United States than in diverse Europe, where the European elections are spread over 27 separate countries.

In short, a lack of homogeneity, contrary to all apparent evidence and ostensible rationality, may well prove conducive to and invigorating for the common good. Following the example of China's *Sanshiliuji* or "Thirty-Six Stratagems" of c. 1500 or the "supra-planning" of Harro von Senger's *Moulüe*, here in Europe too it would be advisable to pay more attention to whether and to what extent the apparent paradox of the antagonistic scenario can be (or, as we have seen, already is being) converted into a homogeneous promotion of a united scenario.[4] The creation of a so-called "stablecoin," i.e. a currency that is stable particularly by comparison with the volatility of Bitcoin, and which is suitable as a common European currency, could perhaps be a fitting model for development that could thereby differentiate itself from the privatization of the monetary system by Facebook's Libra or Amazon Coins.

This Chinese model of "supra-planning" leads effortlessly on to China, which offers a counterpoint to European diversification that is different from the US. In China, the price paid by the individual for the incredible and enormous increase in economic power is exorbitant, and currently reminds us most of the deeply disturbing visions of the future conjured up by Aldous Huxley or George Orwell. The concentration of power that sets all directives lies with the party or its leadership, and the population, i.e. the individual, is exposed to total state surveillance and evaluation by means of "social screening," soon to be in comprehensive use. In private as well as in public, each individual's actions and communications are monitored and subjected to a points account without any kind of notification. When mistakes are made (what kind? running a red light? making critical statements about politics?) points are deducted; in the case of good behavior (what kind? enthusing about the Party? volunteering for military service?) points are earned. Unlike in Flensburg where German motorists can check what traffic offense points they have incurred, this secret points status only has an impact, for example, if you want to get a passport for a foreign trip or a visa—perhaps even when you send your child to school or want to give your child a specific kind of education.

Under such constrained circumstances of uniformity and conformity, Europe's diversity as prescribed merely by multi-nationality seems like a sign of freedom. If we then add the active emphasis on and respect for Christian social teaching, i.e. the recognition of a moral and legal order as a condition of the individual's self-realization, then it seems that the conditions for effectively escaping the forces pulling towards ever-larger entities and power structures, thereby allowing the individual their independent position in society, are most likely to exist in Europe. If these advantages derived from diversity are not only recognized, but even accelerated, there is at least the not entirely unrealistic chance that in many ways this Europe, which has today fallen behind among the big three on this planet, represents the most liveable, and thus most attractive place for many people. Europe might thus be the Reservation that Mustapha Mond, the World Controller for Western Europe in Huxley's *Brave New World*, praises as the one remaining haven that is fit for human beings and thus fit for life.

Notes

1. Brendan Simms, *Europe: The Struggle for Supremacy, 1453 to the Present* (London: Allen Lane, 2013).

2. Josef Joffe, "Träge Riesen" in *Die Zeit*, October 16, 2019, p. 9.

3. Thomas Philippon, *The Great Reversal—How America Gave Up on Free Markets* (Cambridge, MA: The Belknap Press, 2019).

4. Harro Von Senger, *Moulüe—Supraplanung: Unerkannte Denkhorizonte aus dem Reich der Mitte* (Munich: Carl Hanser Verlag, 2018).

CONTRIBUTORS

Dr. Fredrik Erixon is a Swedish economist and writer. He is the Director of the European Centre for International Political Economy (ECIPE), a Brussels-based world-economy think tank which he co-founded in 2006. One of the leading global economy think tanks in the world, ECIPE has been awarded various prizes. Fredrik Erixon is the author of several books in the fields of international economic and regulatory policy, foreign policy, and current affairs, including *The Innovation Illusion* (Yale University Press). Prior to starting ECIPE, Erixon was an adviser to the British government and the Chief Economist of Timbro, a Swedish think tank. He started his career as an economist in the Prime Minister's Office in Sweden and later worked as an economist at the World Bank and for

JP Morgan as an emerging market analyst. Erixon was educated at the University of Oxford, London School of Economics, and Uppsala University.

Prof. Gabriel Felbermayr, Ph.D. is President of the Kiel Institute for the World Economy and holds a Chair in Economics and Economic Policy at Kiel University (CAU). After studying economics and trade at the University of Linz, he went to Florence to pursue his doctoral studies. From 2004 to 2005, he was an Associate Consultant with McKinsey & Co. in Vienna. From 2005 to 2008, he was Assistant Professor at the University of Tübingen. From 2009 to 2010, he held a Chair in International Economics at the University of Hohenheim (Stuttgart). From 2010 to 2019, he led the ifo Center for International Economics at the University of Munich, where he also served as Professor of International Economics. Gabriel Felbermayr is a member of the Scientific Advisory Board of the Germany Federal Ministry of Economics and Energy. He is Associate Editor at the *European Economic Review* and at the *Journal of the European Economic Association*. He has published a large number of papers in international scholarly journals, policy briefs, and newspapers. His research has been recognized with various awards.

Dr. Corinne Michaela Flick studied both law and literature, taking American studies as her subsidiary, at Ludwig Maximilian University, Munich. She gained her Dr. Phil. in 1989. She has worked as in-house lawyer for Bertelsmann Buch AG and Amazon.com. In 1998 she became General Partner in Vivil GmbH und Co. KG, Offenburg. She is Founder and Chair of the Convoco Foundation. As Editor of Convoco! Editions she has published among others: *The Multiple Futures of Capitalism* (Convoco! Editions, 2019), *The Common Good in the 21st Century* (Convoco! Editions, 2018), *Authority in Transformation* (Convoco! Editions, 2017), *Power and its Paradoxes* (Convoco! Editions, 2016), *To Do or Not To Do—Inaction as a Form of Action* (Convoco! Editions, 2015), *Dealing with Downturns: Strategies in Uncertain Times* (Convoco! Editions, 2014), and *Collective Lawbreaking—A Threat to Liberty* (Convoco! Editions, 2013). In 2019 Corinne Flick became the Chair of the Board of Ambassadors at the ESMT Berlin.

Prof. Dr. Birke Häcker holds the statutory Chair in Comparative Law at the University of Oxford. Since her appointment in 2016, she has been a Professorial Fellow at Brasenose College and in 2018 became the Director of Oxford's Institute of European and Comparative Law. Prior to taking up her position, she was, *inter alia*, a Fellow of All Souls College, Oxford, and a Senior Research Fellow at the Max Planck Institute for Tax Law and Public Finance in Munich. As an undergraduate, she obtained a dual legal education, reading jurisprudence at Oxford as well as German law at the Universities of Tübingen and Bonn. Her Oxford D.Phil. was on comparative private law. She publishes on a broad range of topics in English and German private law, comparative law, and legal history.

Dr. Matthias Karl is an expert in European antitrust, competition, and merger law. He has been a partner at law firm Gleiss Lutz since 2000. Matthias Karl studied in Munich, Hamburg, and Ann Arbor, Michigan, USA (LL.M.). He is a member of the German Association for the Study of Antitrust Law, a member of the International Bar Association, and American Bar Association, and on the Antitrust Law Committee of the German Federal Bar Association. Matthias Karl has been a licensed attorney at law in the State of New York, USA, since 1996.

Dr. Parag Khanna is a leading global strategy advisor, world traveler, and best-selling author. He is Founder and Managing Partner of FutureMap, a data- and scenario-based strategic advisory firm. Parag holds a Ph.D. from the London School of Economics, and Bachelors and Masters degrees from the School of Foreign Service at Georgetown University. From 2013 to 2018 he was Senior Research Fellow at the Centre on Asia and Globalisation, National University of Singapore, and in 2006–15 at the New America Foundation. He has been advising many governments and, during 2007, served in Iraq and Afghanistan as a senior geopolitical adviser to the United States Special Operations Forces. Parag has traveled to nearly 150 countries and is a Young Global Leader of the World Economic Forum. He provides regular commentaries for international media, is a contributing editor to *Worldpost,* and serves on the editorial board of *Global Policy.* In 2008 Parag was named one of *Esquire* magazine's "75 Most Influential People of the 21st Century" and featured in *WIRED* magazine's "Smart List." His latest book is *The Future is Asian: Commerce, Conflict & Culture in the 21st Century* (2019).

Prof. Dr. Kai A. Konrad is Director at the Max Planck Institute for Tax Law and Public Finance and a Scientific Member of the Max Planck Society. He was a Full Professor of Economics at the Freie Universität Berlin from 1994 to 2009, and from 2001 to 2009 he was a Director at the Wissenschaftszentrum Berlin für Sozialforschung (WZB). He is a member of the German National Academy of Sciences Leopoldina and of four other science academies. From 2007 to 2018 he was a Co-editor of the *Journal of Public Economics*. Since 1999 he has been a member of the Council of Scientific Advisors to the Federal Ministry of Finance and was the Chair from 2011 to 2014.

Prof. Dr. Stefan Korioth gained his doctorate in law in 1990 and completed his postdoctoral qualification in public and constitutional law. From 1996 to 2000 he was Professor of Public Law, Constitutional History, and Theory of Government at the University of Greifswald. In 2000 he accepted the Chair of Public and Ecclesiastical Law at Ludwig Maximilian University Munich. His publications include *Integration und Bundesstaat* (1990), *Der Finanzausgleich zwischen Bund und Ländern* (1997), *Grundzüge des Staatskirchenrechts* (with B. Jean d'Heur, 2000), *Das Bundesverfassungsgericht* (with Klaus Schlaich, 11th edition, 2018), and *Staatsrecht I – Staatsorganisationsrecht* (4th edition, 2018).

Prof. Dr. Jörn Leonhard is Chair of Western European History at the University of Freiburg, and a prize-winning author. Having studied history, political science, and German philology in Heidelberg and Oxford, he received his Ph.D. in 1998 and completed his post-doctoral qualification at Heidelberg University in 2004. From 1998 to 2003 he was a Fellow and Tutor at Oxford University; Visiting Research Fellow at the *Alexander von Humboldt Foundation in the German–American Center for Visiting Scholars* in Washington, D.C. in 2001; Fellow of the Royal Historical Society London in 2002; and Senior Fellow at the Institute for Contemporary History of the Historisches Kolleg in Munich from 2016 to 2017. From 2007 to 2012 he was Director of the School of History at the Freiburg Institute for Advanced Studies (FRIAS) and in 2012/13 Visiting Professor at Harvard University. His research and publications have received multiple awards. His most recent English publication is *Pandora's Box: A History of the First World War* (2018). Jörn Leonhard has been Honorary Fellow of Wadham College, Oxford University, since 2019.

Prof. Dr. Timo Meynhardt holds the Dr. Arend Oetker Chair of Business Psychology and Leadership at the HHL Leipzig Graduate School of Management. He is Managing Director of the Center for Leadership and Values in Society at the University of St. Gallen, where he obtained his doctorate and postdoctoral qualification in business administration. For several years, he was Practice Expert at McKinsey & Company. Timo Meynhardt's work focuses on public value management, leadership, and competency diagnostics, combining psychology and business management in his research and teaching. He publishes the *Public Value Atlas* for Switzerland and Germany, which aims at making transparent the social benefits of companies and organizations (www.gemeinwohlatlas.de; www.gemeinwohl.ch). His Public Value Scorecard provides a management tool to measure and analyze the creation of public value. He is also Co-founder and Jury Member of the EY Public Value Awards for Startups (www.eypva.com).

Hans Ulrich Obrist (b. 1968, Zürich, Switzerland) is Artistic Director of the Serpentine Galleries in London. Prior to this, he was the Curator of the Musée d'Art Moderne de la Ville de Paris. Since his first show, "World Soup (The Kitchen Show)" in 1991, he has curated more than 300 exhibitions. Obrist has lectured internationally at academic and art institutions, and is a contributing editor to the magazines *Artforum*, *AnOther Magazine*, *032C*, a regular contributor to *Mousse* and *Kaleidoscope*, and he writes columns for *Das Magazin* and *Weltkunst*. In 2011 he received the CCS

Bard Award for Curatorial Excellence, and in 2015 he was awarded the International Folkwang Prize for his commitment to the arts. His recent publications include *Ways of Curating (2015)*, *The Age of Earthquakes* (2015), *Lives of the Artists, Lives of Architects* (2015), *Mondialité* (2017), *Somewhere Totally Else* (2018), and *The Athens Dialogues* (2018).

Dr. Stefan Oschmann is Chairman of the Executive Board and CEO of Merck. Before taking office at the end of April 2016, he served as Vice-Chairman and Deputy CEO, with responsibility for Group Strategy, among other things. Stefan Oschmann joined Merck in 2011 as a member of the Executive Board and was responsible for the healthcare business sector until the end of 2014. He drove the transformation of the biopharma business by optimizing its cost structures and improving the efficiency of its research and development model, which included a clear portfolio prioritization. Before joining Merck, Stefan Oschmann worked for the US pharma company MSD, where he served in a range of senior executive positions. He started his career at an agency of the United Nations, and worked for the German Chemical Industry Association (VCI). Stefan Oschmann was born in Würzburg, Germany in 1957. He holds a doctorate in veterinary medicine from Ludwig Maximilian University in Munich.

Prof. em. Dr. Christoph G. Paulus studied law at Munich, taking his doctorate in law in 1980. His postdoctoral qualification, gained in 1991, was in civil law, civil procedure, and Roman law, for which he was awarded the Medal of the University of Paris II. Between 1989 and 1990 he was a recipient of a Feodor Lynen Stipend from the Humboldt Foundation in Berkeley, from which he had earlier gained his LL.M. From 1992 to 1994 he was Associate Professor at Augsburg, and from the summer semester 1994 he was at the Law Faculty of Humboldt University in Berlin, becoming Dean of the Faculty 2008–10. He is Consultant to the International Monetary Fund and the World Bank. Among other roles, he is a member of the International Insolvency Institute of the American College of Bankruptcy and the International Association for Procedural Law. From 2006 to 2010 he was advisor on insolvency law to the German delegation to UNCITRAL. He is on the editorial board of the *Zeitschrift für Wirtschaftsrecht* (ZIP), the *Northern Annual Review of International Insolvency*, and the *International Insolvency Law Review*.

Prof. Dr. Rupprecht Podszun holds the Chair in Civil Law, German Competition Law, and European Competition Law at Heinrich Heine Universität Düsseldorf and is Director of the university's Institute for Competition Law (IKartR). He has received multiple awards for his outstanding teaching. Since 2013 he has been an Affiliated Research Fellow of the Max Planck Institute for Innovation and Competition in Munich. Previously, Professor Podszun taught at the University of Bayreuth from 2013 to 2016 and was a Visiting Fellow at Cambridge University in 2017. He is Vice-President of the Academic Society for Competition Law (ASCOLA) and runs the blog www.d-kart.de.

H.E. Edi Rama is Prime Minister and Minister of Foreign Affairs of the Republic of Albania and an artist. His diverse career path includes being Professor of Painting at the Albanian Academy of Fine Arts, playing for the national basketball team, and authoring books on his life and art. Edi Rama's involvement in politics started when he was a key leader of the democratic students' movement at the Academy of Fine Arts prior to the dismantling of the communist regime. Following a hiatus of several years in which he left Albania to dedicate himself to his art, Edi Rama re-entered politics in the capacity of the Minister of Culture, Youth, and Sports in 1998. In 2000 Edi Rama was elected Mayor of Tirana Municipality. During his time in office from 2000 to 2011, he transformed and regenerated the capital city. His work found international recognition, including awards such as World Mayor Award (2004) and European Hero Award by *Time* magazine (2005). In 2005 Edi Rama was elected Chair of the Socialist Party of Albania, and he became Prime Minister in 2013 following his parliamentary victory with a center-left coalition. He was re-elected in 2017. Rama remains an active artist and has exhibited his work around the world.

Prof. Jörg Rocholl, Ph.D. is President of ESMT Berlin, Vice-Chair of the advisory board to the German Federal Ministry of Finance and Vice-Chair of the Verein für Socialpolitik (German Economic Association). In addition, Jörg is Research Fellow at the Centre for Economic Policy Research (CEPR), Research Member of the European Corporate Governance Institute (ECGI), Research Professor at the ifo Institute, Chair of the scientific advisory board of the Research Database and Service Center (FDSZ) of Deutsche Bundesbank, Vice-Chair of the economic advisory board of Deutsche Welle, and Member of the scientific advisory board of DIW Berlin. He was both Lamfalussy and Duisenberg Fellow of the European Central Bank. Jörg graduated from Witten/Herdecke University, where he earned a degree in economics (with honors). After completing his Ph.D. at Columbia University in New York, he was named Assistant Professor at the University of North Carolina at Chapel Hill. He has researched and taught at ESMT since 2007 and was appointed President of ESMT in 2011. From 2010 until 2019 he held the EY Chair in Governance and Compliance. His research has been published in leading academic journals.

Prof. Dr. Sven Simon is Chair of International Law, European Law, and Public Law at the Philipps University Marburg and since 2019 a Member of the European Parliament. Born in 1978, he studied law at the Justus Liebig University Gießen and at the University of Warwick, UK. He completed the first state legal examination in 2005 and received his doctorate in 2009. Following his practical legal training in Frankfurt, Berlin, Tel Aviv, and New York, he finished his second state legal examination in 2010. Sven Simon then returned to the Justus Liebig University Gießen to work as Academic Advisor for five years. In 2015 he was awarded his post-doctoral qualification for work on constitutional law analyzing the limits of the German Federal Court in the European integration process. After visiting professorships at the Free University Berlin and the University of Wisconsin, USA, he went on to an appointment at the Philipps University Marburg in 2016. Sven Simon is Deputy Chair of the United Nations Association of Germany.

Prof. Dr. Yael (Yuli) Tamir is the President of Shenkar College in Israel and an Adjunct Professor at the Blavatnik School of Government, Oxford University. Representing the Labor Party, she served as Israel's Minister of Immigration from 1999 to 2001 and as Minister of Education from 2006 to 2009, as well as Deputy Speaker of the Knesset and as a member of various committees. Tamir received her B.A. and M.A. from the Hebrew University in Jerusalem and her Ph.D. in political philosophy from Oxford University, where she wrote her thesis under the supervision of Sir Isaiah Berlin. She was a Professor at Tel Aviv University and a scholar-in-residence at Princeton, Harvard, the European University in Florence, the Central European University in Budapest, NYU, and Penn. Tamir is the author of *Liberal Nationalism* (1993) and *Why Nationalism* (2019), both published by Princeton University Press, and of numerous articles in the fields of moral and political philosophy, philosophy of education, feminism, and human rights. She has received many academic awards for her work. Professor Tamir is a founding member of the Israeli peace movement Peace Now.

Dr. Roberto Viola is Director-General of DG CONNECT (Directorate-General of Communication, Networks, Content, and Technology) at the European Commission. Previously, he was the Deputy Director-General of DG CONNECT from 2012 to 2015 and served as Chairman of the European Radio Spectrum Policy group (RSPG) between 2012 and 2013. He was a member of the BEREC Board (Body of European Telecom Regulators), and Chairman of the European Regulatory Group (ERG). From 2005 to 2012 he held the position of Secretary General in charge of managing AGCOM. Prior to this, he served as Director of Regulation Department and Technical Director in AGCOM from 1999 to 2004. Between 1985 and 1999 he served in various positions, including as Head of Telecommunication and Broadcasting Satellite Services at the European Space Agency (ESA). Roberto Viola holds a Doctorate in Electronic Engineering and a Masters in Business Administration. He has pioneered innovative communication systems, publishing more than 100 scientific papers and holding key patents in the sector.

Prof. Dr. Claudia Wiesner is Jean Monnet Chair and Professor for Political Science at Fulda University of Applied Sciences and Adjunct Professor in Political Science at Jyväskylä University. In spring 2019 she was also Visiting Fellow at the Center for European Studies at Harvard University. Previously, she was Acting Professor for Comparative Politics at Hamburg, Bochum, and Marburg Universities. She has been a Visiting Fellow at the Robert Schumann Centre for Advanced Studies at the European University Institute (EUI), the Berlin Social Sciences Centre, and various international universities. Her main research interests lie in the comparative study of democracy, political culture, and political sociology in the EU multilevel system. Having long-standing experience in public policy consulting, she is also researching the evaluation, reform, and theory of public policy. Wiesner chairs the ECPR Standing Group "Political Concepts" and has led several research projects and international cooperation networks. She has published numerous monographs, book chapters, and journal articles.

THE MULTIPLE FUTURES OF CAPITALISM
2019

ISBN: 978-0-9931953-8-9

With contributions by: Lucio Baccaro, Jens Beckert, Bazon Brock, Corinne M. Flick, Sean Hagan, Kai A. Konrad, Stefan Korioth, Justin Yifu Lin, Rudolf Mellinghoff, Timo Meynhardt, Hans Ulrich Obrist with Adam Curtis, Stefan Oschmann, Christoph G. Paulus, Herbert A. Reitsamer, Albrecht Ritschl, Jörg Rocholl, Gisbert Rühl, Monika Schnitzer, Wolfgang Schön

THE COMMON GOOD IN THE 21st CENTURY
2018

ISBN: 978-0-9931953-6-5

With contributions by: Roland Berger, Bazon Brock, Udo Di Fabio, Carl Benedikt Frey, Clemens Fuest, Kai A. Konrad, Stefan Korioth, Rudolf Mellinghoff, Timo Meynhardt, Hans Ulrich Obrist with Hito Steyerl and Matteo Pasquinelli, Stefan Oschmann, Christoph G. Paulus, Jörg Rocholl, Wolfgang Schön, Jens Spahn

AUTHORITY IN TRANSFORMATION
2017

ISBN: 978-0-9931953-4-1

With contributions by: Claudia Buch, Clemens Fuest, Thomas Hoeren, Peter M. Huber, Kai A. Konrad, Stefan Korioth, Peter Maurer, Hans Ulrich Obrist and Richard Wentworth, Stefan Oschmann, Christoph G. Paulus, Roger Scruton, Wolfgang Schön

POWER AND ITS PARADOXES
2016

ISBN: 978-0-9931953-2-7

With contributions by: Clemens Fuest, Thomas Hoeren, Wolfgang Ischinger, Stefan Korioth, Hans Ulrich Obrist and Simon Denny, Christoph G. Paulus, Albrecht Ritschl, Jörg Rocholl, Roger Scruton, Brendan Simms

TO DO OR NOT TO DO—INACTION AS A FORM OF ACTION
2015

ISBN: 978-0-9931953-0-3

With contributions by: Bazon Brock, Gert-Rudolf Flick, Peter M. Huber, Kai A. Konrad, Stefan Korioth, Friedhelm Mennekes, Hans Ulrich Obrist and Marina Abramović, Christoph G. Paulus, Jörg Rocholl, Wolfgang Schön, Roger Scruton, Pirmin Stekeler-Weithofer

DEALING WITH DOWNTURNS: STRATEGIES IN UNCERTAIN TIMES
2014

ISBN: 978-0-9572958-8-9

With contributions by: Jens Beckert, Bazon Brock, Saul David, Gerd Gigerenzer, Paul Kirchhof, Kai A. Konrad, Stefan Korioth, Christoph G. Paulus, Jörg Rocholl, Burkhard Schwenker

COLLECTIVE LAW-BREAKING—A THREAT TO LIBERTY
2013

ISBN: 978-0-9572958-5-8

With contributions by: Shaukat Aziz, Roland Berger, Christoph G. Paulus, Ingolf Pernice, Wolfgang Schön, Hannes Siegrist, Jürgen Stark, Pirmin Stekeler-Weithofer

WHO OWNS THE WORLD'S KNOWLEDGE?
2012

ISBN: 978-0-9572958-0-3

With contributions by: Eckhard Cordes, Urs Gasser, Thomas Hoeren, Viktor Mayer-Schönberger, Christoph G. Paulus, Jürgen Renn, Burkhard Schwenker, Hannes Siegrist

CAN'T PAY, WON'T PAY? SOVEREIGN DEBT AND
THE CHALLENGE OF GROWTH IN EUROPE
2011

ISBN: 978-0-9572958-3-4

With contributions by: Roland Berger, Howard Davies, Otmar Issing, Paul Kirchhof, Kai A. Konrad, Stefan Korioth, Christoph G. Paulus, Burkhard Schwenker

www.ingramcontent.com/pod-product-compliance
Lightning Source LLC
Chambersburg PA
CBHW020240030426
42336CB00010B/554